MW00414068

CHARLOTTE
TRUE CRIME
STORIES

CHARLOTTE TRUE CRIME STORIES

NOTORIOUS CASES
from Fraud to Serial Killing

Cathy Pickens

THE
History
PRESS

Published by The History Press
Charleston, SC
www.historypress.net

Copyright © 2019 by Cathy Pickens
All rights reserved

First published 2019

Manufactured in the United States

ISBN 9781467142458

Library of Congress Control Number: 2019939734

Notice: The information in this book is true and complete to the best of our knowledge. It is offered without guarantee on the part of the author or The History Press. The author and The History Press disclaim all liability in connection with the use of this book.

All rights reserved. No part of this book may be reproduced or transmitted in any form whatsoever without prior written permission from the publisher except in the case of brief quotations embodied in critical articles and reviews.

To Charlotte—the Queen City—and to her stories, her storytellers and those who preserve them.

A Carolina country road. *Photo by Wes Hicks on Unsplash.*

CONTENTS

CONTENTS

ACKNOWLEDGEMENTS

So many people have helped make this book:

* The amazing staff of the Robinson-Spangler Carolina Room and the Charlotte Mecklenburg Library, particularly Shelia Bumgarner, the Robinson-Spangler Carolina Room librarian. She is a strong advocate for protecting the visual and historical record of Charlotte's history and making it available to those curious about the past.

* The writers and photographers who have covered Charlotte's history and told its stories in newspapers, blogs, television news, documentaries, websites, books and other venues.

* What's a writer without writer friends? Thanks to those who read this book in various stages and who continually encourage my projects: Daniel (Chipp) Bailey, happily retired from "sheriff-ing"; Paula Connolly, Ann Wicker, Dawn Cotter and Terry Hoover, all Really Mean Women; Allison Fetterman; John Jeter; Jeremy Bishop; the merry crew at Charlotte Lit; and Landis Wade and his Charlotte Readers Podcast.

* The team at The History Press who made this project happen, especially editors Kate Jenkins and Sara Miller.

* And always, my husband, Bob; my sisters; and my dad.

1

THE HORNET'S NEST

STATISTICS OR STORIES?

Charlotte has always kept an eye on its place on the national stage while, at the same time, maintaining its sense of humor. Typically, civic leaders only talk about crime in its absence, but in a 1940 *Charlotte News* editorial, the writer took the FBI—and J. Edgar Hoover, personally—to task for snubbing Charlotte and robbing it of its honors as the nation's murder capital, beating out Atlanta ("its ancient rival for first honors").

"As we recall it," pointed out the editorial writer, with tongue poked into his cheek, "the town was at least seven times as murderous as Chicago and ten times as murderous as New York." Yet the annual FBI crime statistics reported that year gave "neither hide nor hair of mention of Charlotte. We couldn't believe our eyes."

Putting the blame firmly on Hoover's desk, the editor wrote, "The man not only has no feeling for the proper pride of a city, he has no sense of drama, either."

Charlotte has always enjoyed a proper pride and a dash of drama. The region has historically been a safe, pleasant place to live but has had its moments in the national crime spotlight and was once dubbed "Little Chicago" in a 1961 *Charlotte News* headline.

By 1966, Charlotte had achieved the ultimate crime-status pinnacle: number one in the nation in murders per 100,000 residents, with almost three times the national average. That year, Charlotte had thirty-seven homicides;

Mecklenburg County's fifth courthouse (in operation from 1928 to 1978), located at 610 East Trade Street, was in use when the city's murder rate hit number one in the nation. *Courtesy of Robinson-Spangler Carolina Room, Charlotte Mecklenburg Library.*

to compare, there were eighty-seven in 2017—Charlotte's seventh-deadliest year. Twenty years earlier, Charlotte had been number two in the national murdering ranks.

Statistics—good ones and bad ones—fluctuate over time, and not always with clear reasons for the ways people can go wrong. Comparison statistics seldom give a clear answer as to whether we're safe or what causes spikes and lulls in crime. Still, we look for explanations and rationales.

In 1977, the police compiled Charlotte's crime data to create an "average" murderer: "A man who uses a pistol and kills somebody he knows during an argument at a residence between 10 and 11 on Saturday night." That description summarizes, with fair accuracy, more recent crime statistics; so, while it may seem like things change, they really don't.

Those regularly reported "annual statistics" or "average" stories seldom grab headlines—or imaginations—for long. So, what makes a story become part of the warp and weft woven into the essence of a city and the people who call it home?

These are the Charlotte stories that started in dark places but show the heart of a city that is still southern and, in good ways, a bit like a small town. These are Charlotte's headline crimes—the stories too important to forget.

THE ORIGINAL NEST

Charlotte started as a crossroads. The area's first public building, erected in 1766—before Charlotte became a town in 1768—was a courthouse, encouraging others to recognize the settlement's respect for law and order, its centrality and its sensibility, though it had fewer than twenty houses.

Soon after, in the Revolutionary War, family and friends faced each other in the Carolinas, where comparatively few British regular troops were stationed. Fleeing losses in Charleston and Camden, British general Lord Cornwallis overtook the Continentals in the Waxhaws (now Lancaster County) just south of Charlotte.

In 1780, the Battle of the Waxhaws (or Buford's Massacre, depending on which side was telling the story) took place forty miles south of the crossroads. The Patriots surrendered. How it turned into a bloody massacre was open to dispute. Banastre Tarleton, the British officer in command, lay pinned under his horse and reportedly had nothing to do with the order to shoot. The Patriots had a different story. The cairn where 150 Continental soldiers were buried stands outside Lancaster in the Buford community named for Virginia officer Abraham Buford. After that skirmish, "remember Tarleton's quarter" came to mean "take no prisoners." The locals were riled.

Four months later, Cornwallis took Charlotte. Charlotte's residents were none too happy with the occupation forces, especially as news of the massacre spread. Local antipathy turned into acts of sabotage, and Cornwallis reportedly wrote that Charlotte was "a hornet's nest of rebellion." Though Cornwallis's letter has not been found, and some count it as rumor, the description stuck.

Charlotte embraced and celebrated its irksome reputation—the Charlotte Hornets basketball team is just one commemoration. Another recognition was Officer E.C. Burgess's design for the police department badge in 1962. Even longtime Charlotte residents may not have studied the emblem on Charlotte-Mecklenburg Police Department vehicles and uniform patches and badges and likely don't recognize the swirling blue-and-white oval as a hornet's nest.

Hornet's nest patch used on Charlotte-Mecklenburg police officers' uniforms. *Sketch by Cathy Pickens.*

When the separate Charlotte Police and Mecklenburg County Police combined into a single force in 1993, both departments agreed on using the hornet's nest. According to CMPD's website, "In the patch, the smaller nest within the larger nest symbolizes growth, while the movement in design suggests motion and change toward a new direction."

THE MOCCA CASE

Those new directions haven't always been simple or easy. In September 2016, following the shooting of Keith Lamont Scott by an officer of the Charlotte-Mecklenburg Police Department, uptown Charlotte saw protestors and police in riot gear and the governor declaring a state of emergency. Few realized that this wasn't Charlotte's first racially divided riot.

News reports from almost 130 years ago show how crime reporting and the community response to crime has changed, and how the city has changed, often in ways we might not expect.

From the end of the Civil War and into the turn of the next century, Charlotte was a remarkably mixed-race southern city. Charlotte historian Tom Hanchett observed, "Segregation had to be invented." Until the Jim Crow laws mandated divides not along class lines but along racial lines, blacks and whites all lived together uptown, with black- and white-owned homes and businesses side by side.

In 1891, John Mocca, an Italian fruit vendor, had a store at the corner of Poplar and Trade Streets, near where the Carillon Building stands today. Between 11:00 p.m. and midnight on Saturday, April 14, he was bludgeoned in what the *Charlotte Democrat* described as "one of the most brutal, cowardly, quiet, and at the same time, daring murders in the annals of crime"—referring not just to crime annals in Charlotte but to all crime annals.

The Italian fruit-seller's murderer, a "negro gambler from Charleston" named Henry Bradham, was under arrest by 10:00 a.m. the next day, which was a Sunday morning. "All day Sunday the city wore a serious demeanor." The talk was of lynching, the paper reported.

Bradham had been in town for a few weeks and was "known as a professional gambler in Charleston, Savannah, and Atlanta…and was hanging around Mocca's store all day" on the day of the murder.

The news account goes into great detail about the Hornet's Nest Riflemen on guard at the jail, sent by the mayor to protect the prisoner and

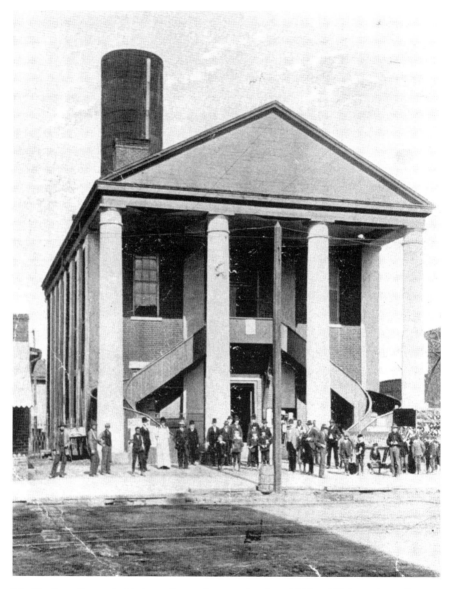

Mecklenburg County's third courthouse (in operation from 1845 to 1896) was located on West Trade Street. *Courtesy of Robinson-Spangler Carolina Room, Charlotte Mecklenburg Library.*

the gatherings of blacks at their nearby church and of whites in the streets. Tempers rose. Two or three hundred shots were fired. Somehow, no one was killed. One white man was shot in the leg.

The news report said: "Judge Means, in his charge to the grand jury and the citizens Monday said the majesty of the law must be vindicated, if the authorities had to wade through blood to do it."

Sheriff Z.T. Smith told the crowd gathered at the jail "that they would have to walk over his 'dead body to lynch that negro.' He is one of the nerviest men in the state and the boys are afraid of him. All idea of lynching has been abandoned."

John Mocca was buried at Elmwood Cemetery "on a lot purchased and donated to deceased's family by Mr. Garibaldi." Mr. Garibaldi was not further identified.

No matter the color of the accused's skin, justice was swift in those days. Three months after the murder, Bradham was tried and hanged "in the jail corridor." On July 3, 1891, the Methodist Episcopal church's reverend, Mr. Austin, spoke for Bradham, saying he'd confessed and he "adjured" other young men to stay away from gambling.

The tradition of gallows confessions is a long one. In England, published pamphlets featuring confessions gave lurid details of crimes (which ensured the pamphlets enjoyed robust sales) and pleas that others would learn from their mistakes (which likely had little influence).

In Charlotte, the newspaper summary was shorter than the old-fashioned English broadsides and omitted the lurid details of the crime, which, of course, limited reader interest in the news report.

Charlotte has grown rapidly, and growing pains can be tough on a city. In fact, growing pains can feel like too-tight shoes as a fairly homogeneous, smallish southern farming and trading town transitions to become a national banking center and a draw for international residents.

Charlotte has always been full of civic boosterism. Its leaders and citizens have, for the most part, been proud of Charlotte. For that reason, sometimes the sketchy parts have been covered over instead of discussed. At one point, a chief of police reportedly forbade officers from mentioning the word "gangs," as if erasing the word would erase the existence of gangs. But why ignore our crime stories? Those stories helped shape the city, and the victors—victims and villains alike—are woven into the fabric of the city.

CHARLOTTE'S FAMOUS CASES

Charlotte has several nationally known cases I won't explore in detail, because good accounts appear in other History Press books—see *Wicked Charlotte: The Sordid Side of the Queen City* by Stephanie Burt Williams (2006) and *Charlotte: Murder, Mystery and Mayhem* by David Aaron Moore (2008). These cases deserve at least a quick mention.

PTL

When Charlotte's NationsBank acquired California-based Bank of America in 1998, Charlotte became the second-largest financial center in the United States. While the banking industry has hosted its own frauds and failures of judgment, those tend to lack the flair of some of our homegrown financial fandangos. A city would find it hard to claim kin with PTL or the Loomis Fargo "gang who couldn't shoot straight" without a firm hold on its sense of humor.

Mention "fraud" around Charlotte, and those who know the city's history will immediately think of PTL (Praise the Lord) and Jim and Tammy Faye Bakker. In the mid-1980s, the couple's religious broadcasts, Christian theme park and residential retreat put their 2,500-acre center, which was located five miles southeast of Carowinds, on the map. They built one of the most recognizable Christian retreats in the country, much of it patterned on the Disney parks. They then presided over its slide into ignominy amidst charges of financial fraud against "partners" who invested in a resort hotel with five hundred rooms (including one hundred honeymoon suites, where couples could come to recharge their marriages).

When rumors of Jim Bakker's sexual impropriety with a church secretary in a hotel in Florida were substantiated and the lavish lifestyle of the Bakkers was uncovered (an air-conditioned doghouse and gold-plated bathroom fixtures featured prominently in television and newspaper coverage), the Bakkers resigned. The downfall was swift.

Accusations that PTL vacation rentals had been oversold and monies misused led to a federal criminal prosecution, a fraud conviction and a prison sentence for Jim Bakker, the preacher who started it all.

Long before the criminal investigation, jokes around Charlotte (and elsewhere) changed the name of the ministry from the Praise the Lord Club to the "Pass the Loot" Club.

Commercial National Bank, founded in 1874, was the predecessor of Bank of America. *Courtesy of Robinson-Spangler Carolina Room, Charlotte Mecklenburg Library.*

In 2019, the empty, never-completed twenty-one-story Heritage Towers Hotel could still be seen from vantage points miles away in south Charlotte—an unusual testament to an aberrant intersection of Charlotte's roots in finance and religion.

Loomis Fargo Heist

One of the largest armored car heists in history was plotted in 1997 at a Gaston County cookout over beer and burgers. It was only the second-largest armored-car heist Loomis suffered in that one year, but the theft of $17 million was enough to win it the seventh-place slot on the list of largest heists in world history (as of 2016). The stunning size of the heist was eclipsed by the good-old-boy tone of the caper. It holds the honor of being the only Charlotte financial crime to provide the creative spark for a comic movie: *Masterminds* (2016), starring Zach Galifianakis, Owen Wilson and Kristen Wiig.

In an essay in *27 Views of Charlotte*, I offered a "note for would-be bank robbers: take the money and leave your hometown. Moving from your mobile home into a $635,000 country club house attracts attention, especially if you pay cash. So does paying for a minivan in $20 bills and asking bank tellers how much money you can deposit without filling out government paperwork."

Rae Carruth

Charlotte was thrilled when the city won an NFL franchise for its Carolina Panthers, as it offered evidence that the city was grown-up. The aerial views televised during Sunday games showed the nation a gleaming southern centerpiece of a city.

When first-round draft pick Rae Carruth landed Charlotte on *Court TV* in 1999, it televised another view of a city both mesmerized and embarrassed by the story. Carruth allegedly didn't want to pay child support, so he got career criminal Van Brett Watkins and two other men to pull up beside his pregnant girlfriend's BMW, shoot into her car and kill her and the baby.

Carruth's girlfriend, Cherica Adams, lived long enough to let police know what happened. Watkins pled guilty, and in riveting courtroom testimony, he said Rae was there, blocking Adams's car so they could pull beside her.

The baby survived but battled challenges that resulted from his difficult birth. Raised by his grandmother, he became a remarkable young man with a big smile and an inner fight that won him fans to rival the number who used to cheer his father on game day.

The case reminded Charlotte that big money and bright lights can attract and highlight the best and the worst of what we can become.

MY FAVORITE CASES

Razor Girl

Two of my favorite Charlotte cases reflect much that fascinates me about Charlotte. The first is the story of Razor Girl. I wrote about her in *27 Views*:

> *I first learned of Razor Girl's 1926 case visiting a Charlotte-Mecklenburg Police exhibit at the Museum of History in 2010. No historical crime review of a Southern city can overlook a case that so neatly highlighted the privilege of being a murderess in an older South, at least if you were small and funny and knew how to flirt.*
>
> *True, her 23-year-old bigamist husband Alton Freeman was, as we say, no better than he ought to be. He'd been running around on her, a convicted thief living off her $15-a-week factory wages. One night, he told his nineteen-year-old wife Nellie he was leaving her as soon as he pulled off a whiskey heist.*
>
> *Nellie calmly told the officer who later arrived at their little house that she'd hugged him around the neck, asking if he didn't love her. He didn't. She didn't know how sharp the knife was, she said, until he lay on the floor, only a bit of flesh and bone holding his head to his body.*
>
> *Nellie wasn't shy about talking to police and to newspapers. She attracted the best lawyers in town to her defense team. Charlotte juries had a habit of acquitting women of murder, and prosecutor and former mayor Frank McNinch vowed he'd see the end of women getting away with murder. The battle was set.*
>
> *The courtroom was packed every day of the trial. Women in particular flocked to see the spectacle. After all, a woman couldn't be sent to prison, could she? That wasn't the done thing. All that was missing was a cotton candy vendor, but someone was selling replica straight razor pins to commemorate the event.*

Left: Nellie Freeman, nicknamed "Razor Girl" in the press, at the time of her trial. *Sketch by Cathy Pickens.*

Below: A 1926 North Tryon street scene shows city hall on the right, a trolley and department stores. *Courtesy of Robinson-Spangler Carolina Room, Charlotte Mecklenburg Library.*

The all-male jury for Nellie Freeman's murder trial. *Courtesy of* Charlotte Observer *and Charlotte Mecklenburg Library.*

Mecklenburg County's fourth courthouse (in operation from 1896 to 1928), located at the corner of Tryon and Third Streets across from Latta Arcade, during Nellie Freeman's trial. *Courtesy of Robinson-Spangler Carolina Room, Charlotte Mecklenburg Library.*

> *The jury deliberated for two days, read some Bible verses on forgiveness, talked the manslaughter hold-outs around, and found Nellie Freeman not guilty by reason of insanity, it being not unheard of that a woman could be "struck crazy" for a short period of time, long enough to kill a lying, cheating husband. The judge allowed her to take her bloodied dress and her razor with her, and she seems to have vanished from Charlotte headlines.*

She didn't vanish from Charlotte forever, though. Journalist David Aaron Moore found that she soon returned to Charlotte with a new husband. She settled into a quiet and seemingly happy life in the Enderly Park neighborhood and was married for forty years before she died at Mercy Hospital in 1964 at age sixty-nine. Charlotte has changed over the course of the last hundred years, and Nellie reminds us how much.

Bigfoot

Another of my favorite stories isn't about a crime at all—just a bit of "gotcha." Philip Morris of Morris Costumes created illusions that reached far beyond Charlotte.

In the 1950s, Morris arrived in Charlotte for a performance and, as so many visitors have, decided to stay. He worked with creative passion and built a business with a national reach. One of his creations, in particular, sparked intrigue and controversy.

Morris Costumes on Monroe Road is more than a great place for Halloween shopping. Philip Morris, a magician and former ringmaster with the Royal Hanneford Circus with an infectious joy of life, started making gorilla costumes for an act that was once a staple in traveling carnival sideshows: beautiful girl transforms into rampaging gorilla.

Morris's other show-business creations included an animated suit for a Wisconsin theme park modeled on Gargantua, who toured with Ringling Bros. and Barnum & Bailey Circus in the 1930s and 1940s. He also created the white gorilla suit used in the James Bond movie *Diamonds Are Forever*, and he settled a lawsuit with the producers of the *Austin Powers* movies over the name Dr. Evil, a character Morris created for Charlotte television in 1959.

His basement business grew from hawking gorilla suits to becoming the world's largest costume distributor. I met him one October night at his too–short-lived Halloween haunted house attraction behind his Monroe Road store. The display showcased equipment and costumes he sold to haunted

The home of the internationally known Morris Costumes on Monroe Road. *Photo by Libby Dickinson.*

attractions around the country, all gathered in a delightful array. My husband and I were the oldest visitors on the lot at the time, so he approached us, leaning in with a conspiratorial air: "How do you like it?"

His signature smile (the one that often appeared, beaming, inside one of his costumes in his Halloween ads) creased his face as he told us how his grandson didn't like haunted houses—until he gave him a costume and let him be a part of the scaring. "Now, he loves it! Wants to know when he can do it again!" Who wouldn't?

Morris's most controversial story circled back around to gorillas and the suit Morris made for Roger Patterson in 1967—the costume reportedly used in the famous video footage, created by Patterson and Bob Gimlin, of Bigfoot (or Sasquatch) strolling through a California forest.

After getting the costume, Patterson called Morris to ask for ways to make the costume move more realistically. "Use a stick to extend the arms, brush the fur to cover the zipper and wear football pads to make the shoulders bigger," was his response, Morris told *Observer* reporter Tonya Jameson in 2004. Morris had known nothing about Patterson's planned film and didn't talk to Patterson again.

Morris said he didn't talk about his connection with the famous suit until after Patterson died, and then only to insiders in the illusion and entertainment business. As a magician, he wasn't one to destroy another illusionist's trick.

The story eventually moved outside the inner circle of his family, friends and trade colleagues when Greg Long learned about it and interviewed Morris for his book *The Making of Bigfoot: The Inside Story*. Long said Morris's story agreed with details given by Bob Heironimus, the man identified as the wearer of the suit for the film.

Of course, cryptozoologists (those who study "hidden animals" such as the Loch Ness monster and Sasquatch) decry Long's book and the attempts to debunk the Patterson/Gimlin footage. Morris, who died in 2017 at age eighty-three, would likely flash his signature grin and shrug. Who knew gorilla suits better than he did?

Whether illusory or real, ridiculed by others or baked into the bricks and mortar of our civic character, Charlotte's stories—good and bad, heroic or tragic—often carry at their heart a sense of community…and, sometimes, of impish good fun.

WHY THESE CASES?

I can't claim to be from Charlotte; I moved from South Carolina hill country in the early 1980s, and where I come from, you're not "from" there unless you were born in that place. Charlotte lacked that insularity and still welcomes travelers at its crossroads. Interlopers like me now outnumber the natives. Though I'll always feel my "newcomer" status, I've spent decades here with a raconteur's respect for the power stories have to reveal things about a place and its people.

The following are cases that, for me, reflect the Charlotte I've watched over the years and include crimes of all sorts. I followed most of these cases as they unfolded in the newspaper and on the evening news. The first reporter on the scene at the Outlaws massacre became a friend. Kim Thomas's house was only a few blocks up the road from mine. I've gotten to know reporters, defense lawyers, prosecutors, police officers, crime scene techs and a sheriff or two who've all been on the front lines of these cases.

Though Charlotte is officially a "big city," it still has its small-town roots, and those who are missing or murdered may seem like someone we know in that intimate, small-town way of knowing and caring. They are part of Charlotte, and those who listen for the city's stories feel their loss.

Throughout its history, from its hornet's nest logo to its Hugo the Hornet basketball mascot and its commemorative straight-razor pins, Charlotte also has maintained a wry sense of humor and appreciation for the offbeat or out-of-step. That may be my favorite part of Charlotte and its history.

This book is not a work of investigative journalism. The information is solely drawn from published or broadcasted resources, including newspapers, television documentaries, podcasts, books, print and online magazine articles and scholarly papers.

One of the dangers inherent in recounting historical events is that accounts vary. Some reported "facts" aren't accurate—or are at odds with someone else's memory or perception of the event. While I have worked to present as many points of view as possible, I'm sure there are mistakes. My apologies in advance.

These stories, drawn from the layers of Charlotte's older self and the people coming in or passing through, offer glimpses at the rich complexity of the hornet's nest and how people, facing the worst moments of their lives, kept their proper pride and their humor.

TRICKSTERS, FRAUDS AND MURDER

Con artists and financial fraudsters certainly aren't new or unique to Charlotte, but Charlotte's tricksters offer their own hometown twists.

SOUTHERN CHARMER AND SPY: GASTON MEANS

The Charlotte region's most colorful fraudster rarely gets the attention he deserves—attention he undoubtedly would have enjoyed. Among textbook fraud cases, the one that elevated Charlotte's status early in the twentieth century took place largely in New York City, but the perpetrator was a homegrown boy, born in Concord (twenty-five miles northeast of Charlotte), who made good use of his slow drawl and dimple-cheeked charm.

The case is also a textbook lesson that large-scale fraud wasn't invented in the internet age: Gaston Bullock Means was born in 1879.

His father was a Concord lawyer with a good enough reputation to represent Cannon Mills as business took off for its "Turkish" toweling. As a child, Gaston had reportedly helped his dad with his court cases, eavesdropping on conversations around town to see how the men on the street—including jurors—might be leaning in a particular case.

Following an accepted path for well-to-do young men, Gaston Means attended the University of North Carolina and was, for a time, a teacher and a superintendent of education in Albemarle (forty miles east of Charlotte) before he switched careers.

Gaston B. Means, southern charmer and spy, on trial. *Courtesy of Library of Congress, Prints & Photographs Division, LC-USZ62-102198.*

He headed to New York in 1902 to sell towels and textiles for Kannapolis's growing Cannon Mills. And he was a successful salesman, soon earning $5,000 per year—equivalent to about $150,000 in 2018.

What transformed him from a man living a settled, predictable life just outside Charlotte to a skilled salesman to "the greatest faker of them all" isn't clear. Was the con artist always there? Or did he start as a gifted teacher, spinning captivating stories for his students, before finding that he had a larger gift for telling stories so big that people shouldn't believe him—but did? His life's path suggests that he genuinely enjoyed getting people to believe the unbelievable.

At six feet tall and over two hundred pounds, Gaston Means was imposing, though he was bald and soft. Judging from his photograph, Gaston doesn't seem likely as a lady-killer. But his southern accent, charm and ability to spin elaborate and convincing tales must have been attractive to both men and women.

As befits a talented con artist, some parts of his chronology are hard to piece together, but in 1911, he left what he had turned into a very lucrative job selling towels and made an unpredictable career move. He went to work for William J. Burns, head of the International Detective Agency and chief competitor of the Pinkerton Agency.

This was a time when public police forces were small or nonexistent, and with the growth of business and travel across state and international lines, those who needed law enforcement turned to private detectives.

Starting in the 1800s with François Vidocq (who went from being a French criminal to founding the first police force), as police forces began to develop, the line between crooks and cops could be thin indeed. Within both France's Sûreté Nationale and England's Bow Street Runners (started in 1749 by magistrate and novelist Henry Fielding), the initial police forces drew from those who knew crime best: men who had been criminals.

For reasons that are not quite clear, given what's known of his background, Gaston Means fit in quite nicely with the play-close-to-the-edge-of-the-law culture of the Burns Agency. For Means, maybe it was just a logical shift from salesman to adventurer to criminal.

On one of his assignments, he worked for the German government at the start of World War I, reporting on armament shipments to Britain. The ethics of providing information to help German U-boats find their targets didn't seem to concern either William Burns or Gaston Means. The United States wasn't yet involved in the war, and the men were not breaking any laws. Plus, the Germans paid extremely well for the information; Secret

Charlotte's skyline in 1911 (the year Gaston Means joined Burns's International Detective Agency), featuring city hall, Realty Building and Selwyn Hotel. *Courtesy of Robinson-Spangler Carolina Room, Charlotte Mecklenburg Library.*

Agent E-13 may have earned $100,000 a year from the Germans. When the United States entered the war, Means then worked for Allied interests, though it didn't pay as well.

Postwar work seems to have shifted his ethical base more dramatically than any other step on his path. In 1917, the Burns Agency assigned him the case of Maude A. King, the widow of a Chicago man who had made his money in lumber. She had become the target of a group of Monte Carlo swindlers who were draining her dry.

Means, oozing southern charm, stepped in to rescue her—and to further relieve her of the burden of the money her husband had left her.

Her husband, James King, had (quite wisely, as it turned out) left her only a portion of his fortune. Maude King had an annual income of $70,000—the equivalent of almost $2 million in 2018. This was a generous portion, to be sure, but it was not sufficient for the likes of Gaston Means. The bulk of James King's multimillion-dollar estate (at the time, reports put it somewhere between $3 and $10 million) was held tantalizingly out of reach in a trust for charitable work.

That was no barrier for a determined Means. He forged a new will for James King and presented it to the court for probate; its later (fake) date set aside the true will and give all the funds to Maude King.

Gaston then invited Maude down home to Concord, where she could have some important paperwork handled for her. While there, Gaston proposed a night hunt—some said for rabbits, some said for target practice. Apparently, this woman who'd always been afraid of guns had, under the charming influence of Gaston Means, decided that a southern night hunt sounded like fun. According to Means, he placed a gun in the crook of a tree and told her not to touch it. She touched it and managed to shoot herself in the head—the back of the head, according to accounts.

He carried her (as southerners would say) into town, where she died of her wounds. Suspicions were raised (of course), questions were asked about the absence of gunshot residue around the wound (indicating that the gun was held too far away for her to have shot herself) and Means was indicted and tried for murder in Concord.

His defense counsel pointed out that outsiders from up North were persecuting this local boy. On December 16, 1916, after a short deliberation, the jury acquitted Means.

Means went back to work for the Burns Agency. In 1921, Burns was appointed by President Warren G. Harding's attorney general to run the FBI. Burns hired Means to join him. Now working for the government, they continued business as usual. Means found that his FBI position offered a lucrative side business selling "protection" to bootleggers during Prohibition.

Harding's administration was rife with corruption and at least two suicides, and it finally exploded in the Teapot Dome scandal.

Means often claimed to be deep in the inner circle, receiving assignments directly from the president, but that was likely another of his outlandish tales. Regardless of the details, Means's tale-spinning carried him to increasingly dangerous heights, and he was caught up in the multiple investigations around Harding.

The ledger accounts were stacking up against Means. In his role as a political fixer, Means got himself involved in the Glass Coffin Case in 1922. The concept of glass coffins excited an investment company in New York, and sales were brisk. Unfortunately, the coffin company was better at selling its concept than it was at scheduling the manufacture and delivery of actual glass coffins. Even in the days ahead of the 1929 stock-market crash, this sort of exuberant overselling was frowned upon and eventually attracted prosecutorial attention.

Means, from his lofty perch in the Justice Department, assured the principals and their lawyers—what the government later called "the casket crowd"—that he could take care of their legal concerns…for a price. The $65,000 bribe (the equivalent of over $900,000 in 2018) ended up being divided into so many hands that Means couldn't have benefitted much by the deal. And though he might be able to stop a federal case, he had no control over the state prosecutors who filed charges. The case eventually blew up, shattering the dreams of a glass-coffin empire.

Means was with his wife, Julie, and son in a big Union Street house in Concord when officers came to take him to Charlotte and, from there, by train to New York, where he was convicted and sentenced to two years in the Atlanta federal penitentiary.

Even the judge, writing the court opinion when one of Means's codefendants appealed, seemed to be shaking his head over the whole affair: "In some curious way they [the coffin crowd] thought themselves unjustly treated, because they had paid out so much money and then been indicted after all."

A time as a full-fledged international man of mystery, followed by a modestly successful bout of fleecing a rich, impressionable widow and dodging a murder charge, capped by a flamboyant fling in a wildly corrupt presidential administration, would be an outstanding legacy for most con men. But it wasn't quite enough for Gaston Means.

While in the Atlanta penitentiary, he made the acquaintance of *True Confessions* writer May Dixon Thacker, who helped him write an exposé claiming President Harding had been poisoned by his wife as revenge for his well-known affair with Nan Britton. As with most of Means's elaborate tales, this one had enough detail to lend credence; the frontispiece of her book is a letter from Means to Thacker typed on stationery from the Herald Square Hotel in New York, attesting that "it has been constantly my purpose and intention to show to you undisputable documentary evidence verifying any and all statements that I have made to you." Means further said he did not intend for Thacker "at any time, to publish any statement of mine that I am unable to verify myself with undisputable, self-evident documentary evidence." The letter identified him as an "ex–Department of Justice investigator."

Of course, the resulting book, *The Strange Death of President Harding*, sold well. By this time, Means had served his full sentence in the Glass Coffin Case and was released in July 1928, but he was still broke.

So, he concocted perhaps his wildest scheme: to convince the wealthy Evalyn Walsh McLean to pay the ransom for the kidnapped baby of Charles Lindbergh. He'd known the socialite McLean—owner of the Hope Diamond—from his time in the Harding administration. He offered to serve as a go-between, carrying the $100,000 ransom she was willing to pay. She was most anxious to help rescue the Lindberghs' baby, so she withdrew the money and drove to her vacation home in Aiken, South Carolina, as Means instructed.

The kidnappers, through Means, sent her on confusing cross-country roundabouts more difficult to follow than the hands of a street-corner card hustler. Eventually, a suspicious friend of McLean's came to Means and demanded the return of the money.

"What? She didn't get it? I returned it to her messenger, as arranged!"

Means's last criminal prosecution commenced shortly thereafter.

Gaston Means died in 1938—not quite fifty years old, with a bad heart and kidney problems—in the federal penitentiary medical facility in Leavenworth, leaving a long trail from Concord, North Carolina.

Means appeared as a character in television's *Boardwalk Empire*, as a fast and loose Department of Justice investigator, so not everyone has forgotten his immense talents. His time at the Justice Department was a small part of his career, but, after all, who would believe a hometown schoolteacher acquitted of killing a woman he'd defrauded, who spied for the Germans, swindled a woman into thinking she could recover the Lindbergh baby and wrote a book "proving" a president's wife poisoned him because he had an affair?

WHEN GREED TURNS DEADLY: JOEY CALDWELL

Fraud cases that make headlines are interesting but can be hard to follow if the facts are complex, convoluted and contested while the solution takes time to unfold.

At first, the April 12, 1991 shotgun murders of a mother and son, eighty-three-year-old Vela and forty-four-year-old Maceo (MAY-see-o) McEachern (ma-KAY-han), were pure mystery and not easily solved. Who could want to kill these pillars of Hamlet, North Carolina? Two days after the murders, a *Charlotte Observer* article opened with the words "With few clues and a trail growing colder…"

But, Hamlet chief of police Terry Moore was known to be a methodical man, one to shut himself in his office and study files until he shook something loose—in this case, he uncovered a twisted tale of fraud.

At first glance, the solution could have been a simple break-in, a random tragedy, but police quickly ruled out robbery, leaving three other avenues to explore: a $2 million business lawsuit in which Maceo was to be a star witness, other business conflicts or romantic or personal conflicts.

Maceo's friends around Hamlet knew that his love life could be complicated. He was a ladies' man, but he also had a constant, long-term girlfriend who'd stood by him. Naturally, police had to ask questions about romantic entanglements, but that led nowhere.

So, the investigation focused on his business interests, which quickly took investigators two hours away, to Charlotte and Belmont, North Carolina, where they untangled knotted threads of greed to reveal a very methodical, planned execution rather than a random tragedy.

The McEachern mother and son ran funeral homes in both Hamlet and nearby Rockingham. Maceo's father, Maceo D., had started the business, and Vela, when she retired from teaching, joined him as a hands-on partner in running it. When her husband became ill, she eventually took over, and Maceo got licensed and joined his mother in running the family funeral homes, though that had not been his life's ambition.

Mother and son were close; he lived part of the time at her house, but he also kept an apartment at the mortuary and visited his long-time girlfriend, Naomi Daggs. The McEacherns were well-to-do, with a spacious brick ranch in the McEachern Forest neighborhood at the nexus between traditionally black and white neighborhoods in Hamlet. The McEacherns crossed other barriers, too: Maceo, an outgoing, personable man described as a "quick-witted bear of a man," had been elected a Richmond County

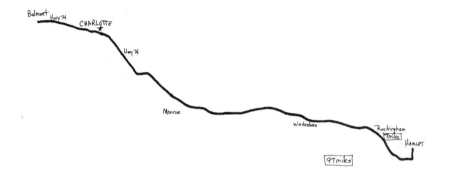

Above: Map showing Hamlet, Rockingham, Belmont and Charlotte. *Sketch by Cathy Pickens.*

Left: The McEacherns pictured on the cover of *Deadly Greed* by Clark Cox. *Courtesy of Canterbury House Publishing.*

commissioner and, later, to the school board. In addition to handling the funeral services at their mortuaries, he bred horses and was deeply involved in the Hamlet community.

But his business success apparently didn't feel like all his own doing. He wanted to establish himself outside the shadow of the family business. Sometimes slow and steady employment isn't enough. Sometimes a man longs for something flashier—a big score, something to prove he's not beholden to his mother or anyone else.

Even with the loftiest ambitions, few business ventures end in murder.

In his book *Deadly Greed*, Clark Cox, a forty-year veteran newspaper writer and editor, took time to personalize the victims and their loved ones. In particular, his interviews with Daggs, an English teacher at Richmond Community College, paint a fully realized picture of Maceo. The resulting portrait shows both the good and the not-perfect parts of Maceo and his family, which takes this case beyond the bare facts into a world populated by people who truly miss the victims and whose lives are lessened because of their loss.

For the public, cases unfold piecemeal as investigators uncover—then reveal or hold close—information, and as reporters dig for what the investigators aren't yet telling. Within days of the deaths, Maceo's involvement with a Charlotte sports-drink company was reported in the press, though Pro-Formance officials couldn't be reached for comment.

The *Charlotte Observer* headlines reported that Maceo was supposed to testify in a $2 million lawsuit. The suit accused Clyde Sullivan, a beer wholesaler who lived in Southern Pines, of fraud and conspiracy, alleging that Sullivan and Maceo tried to gain control of the Pro-Formance company. Maceo had had a change of heart about the takeover attempt and was now a principal witness for the Caldwells, owners of Pro-Formance.

Pro-Formance was Joey Caldwell's latest business venture, a sports drink designed to compete with Gatorade—but better tasting, said Caldwell. He had developed it in 1989 and was selling it to five hundred southeastern outlets. In 1990, Sullivan had contracted with Joey Caldwell and his wife, Bobbie, to be Pro-Formance's exclusive distributor. Caldwell thought having an experienced distributor would put his drink in more outlets. But, according to the lawsuit, Sullivan planned to "squeeze Joey Caldwell out" by refusing to distribute his product until he signed over interest in the company. Instead of delivering product to distributors, Sullivan dried up much of the Caldwells' cash flow and put them in a financial bind. He planned to starve Caldwell to the point that he'd be willing to sell the product rights cheaply.

When Caldwell balked, according to the lawsuit, Sullivan reportedly said he could "call in…Special Forces buddies [who could] take care of somebody and nobody would ever find them."

Caldwell didn't cave, and Sullivan's takeover plan began falling apart. Maceo approached Caldwell himself to work out their own deal. Maceo would buy the rights to the sports drink, with most of the payment coming from future profits. As part of the agreement, the Caldwells took out two life insurance policies on Maceo totaling $2 million and payable to the Caldwells' holding company, Gymbags Inc., to ensure against future royalty losses if something happened to Maceo. The amount far exceeded the current royalty amounts, but they were planning on growth.

Sullivan's attempts to undermine his drink distribution left Joey Caldwell desperate for cash. And Joey would do whatever it took to maintain his lifestyle. Coming from a working-class background, Joey always dreamed of a better life. He'd promised Bobbie, his fourth wife, that he'd be a millionaire by the time he was thirty-five—and he made it. But now, too soon, he was back in debt.

Months after the deaths of the McEacherns, the Caldwells finally collected the $2 million "key man" life insurance payout. They also settled the lawsuit with Sullivan. After all, they'd lost their star witness against Sullivan when Maceo died.

In a January 1993 article published almost two years after the murders, the *Observer* listed the McEachern case as among the North Carolina State Bureau of Investigation's "haunting" unsolved murders. The investigation had consumed months. Investigators were convinced their prime suspect had been seen loitering near the McEacherns' house before the murders— the same man who had two million reasons to stand in their living room and shotgun two people to death. But the case was hard to prove.

The best witness against Joey Caldwell would be his wife, but in a criminal case in a North Carolina state court, a wife could not testify against her husband. Investigators looked for another way to set up the chessboard in what was becoming a tricky game.

Murder is, in most cases, a state crime. The killer had driven a car with a Canadian license tag (stolen, it turned out, from a vacationer in Myrtle Beach). Crossing state lines to commit a felony is a federal offense, so the U.S. attorney's office could enter the case.

Money laundering (such as moving ill-gotten insurance proceeds through bank accounts), mail fraud and weapons violations are federal crimes. In federal courts, a spouse can waive immunity, so a wife could testify against her husband.

Investigators had suspicions about Bobbie. She'd been involved in the business. She had outlined a detailed itinerary of how she and Joey spent the day of the murders in Charlotte, including working out at the YMCA on Morehead Street (proved with their electronic ID cards), buying tickets to see the movie *Class Action* at the Park Terrace Cinemas in Park Road Shopping Center and purchasing toothpaste at Eckerd's near SouthPark Mall.

The alibi was maybe *too* good—until a Charlotte lawyer approached the U.S. attorney to make a "proffer" on behalf of an unnamed client. A proffer, in a legal context, is an offer made on behalf of one side seeking concessions from the other in exchange for information. The client for whom the proffer was made was identified only as Client X, but investigators knew only one person who had the kind of information that was being offered: Bobbie. The legal chessboard was set and ready for play.

Investigators knew Bobbie Caldwell was likely the weak link in the case, but was she also the mastermind? Joey wasn't known as a deep thinker, and their alibi for the day of the murders involved plenty of details. Bobbie could have been hard to crack—except that Joey himself helped the investigators win her over. The Caldwells' debts for their lavish lifestyle and his misbegotten business moves had eaten through most of what they'd collected of the insurance policy on Maceo McEachern's life, so Joey began pushing Bobbie to get an insurance policy on her life.

She didn't fall for that.

Bobbie answered a subpoena to testify before a federal grand jury. Federal grand juries are investigative bodies, and testimony is secret; Joey wouldn't know what she was saying.

However, once she was subpoenaed, Joey Caldwell had enough sense to know he had reason to worry.

Bobbie, too, knew the risk. At that point, the case took a real cloak-and-dagger turn: Bobbie agreed to wear a wire and to get Joey to talk about what happened in Hamlet. She secretly recorded him during dinner at a Chili's restaurant in Gastonia. On the tape, he indicated he would kill himself before he went through a trial. "It's not like I'm willing to go through a trial and all that," he told her.

Joey didn't have a chance to act on that pledge. Officers were monitoring the conversation. He was arrested as he left the restaurant.

Only as testimony unfolded at the trial did newspapers report the more dramatic details of the investigation.

Joey told Bobbie he hated that it had to be Maceo, that he liked Maceo. But the insurance policy made him the logical fall guy when their distributorship failed and the cash flow dried up. The plans were elaborate but doomed, and the results were final and tragic.

As Joey and Bobbie told investigators when first questioned, they had swiped their access cards at the Dowd YMCA on Morehead Street in Charlotte. Their first version veered away from reality at that point. Joey slipped out a side door and left. Nothing at the Y registered how long they stayed or when either of them left, only when they swiped their cards to enter.

Joey drove to Hamlet with the stolen Canadian license tag on the car and tape covering the identifying emblems on his Acura. He hung out at the side of a residential street near the McEacherns' house, which was in a small-town neighborhood where passersby take note of anything unusual.

Meanwhile, Bobbie was back in Charlotte gathering the alibi evidence for both of them. Joey had already watched the movie they allegedly watched at Park Road, so he could talk about it. They'd thought about everything needed to prove they were in Charlotte.

What they hadn't planned on was how unpredictable potential targets could be. Friday, April 12, apparently wasn't the first time they'd scheduled the murder of Maceo McEachern. An earlier attempt failed when Maceo just didn't show up where Joey needed him to be.

Joey hoped he'd have a better shot at Maceo outside the car, before he pulled toward the carport or entered the house, so Joey put a cinder block (stolen from a construction site on Old Dowd Road in Charlotte) in the McEachern's driveway to get Maceo out of his car. Had that not worked? The block puzzled Police Chief Terry Moore for years. He knew the red clay on the block didn't come from the sandy soil around Hamlet. Red clay came from Charlotte.

Those close to the case wondered whether Vela McEachern was collateral damage. Had Joey not been able to get Maceo isolated and outside the car? Did Joey get inside the house and force Vela to lure Maceo back home? Maceo got a phone call from his mother that day as he was working on an embalming job at the Rockingham funeral home. If Joey was in her house, telling her to get Maceo home, for some reason Vela didn't warn Maceo she was being held at gunpoint. Maybe she thought he'd be able to talk to the gunman or overpower him. Maceo had taken care of her for years.

All she had to do was ask. Maceo drove straight home. The next event established by crime scene analysis was that Maceo sat in one of the chairs in his mother's living room and was shot in the mouth. His mother, sitting on the sofa, must have witnessed it. Her hand was raised to ward off the first shot that hit her.

When Maceo didn't return to finish the funeral preparations, a funeral home employee went to check on him. Through the front window, the employee quickly saw that things weren't right.

What the Hamlet police force lacked in size, it made up for in dedication. Hamlet Police chief Terry Moore had been a guest in the McEachern house and had sat in that living room. Now, he had to use his photography skills to capture a crime scene no one in Hamlet would have imagined.

Hamlet wasn't a stranger to homicide. According to journalist Clark Cox, the county of forty-five thousand averaged twelve murders each year—per capita, that's more than many larger cities. But those were the types of murders usually solved quickly: bar fights, drug deals, domestic violence. This case was not so predicable; this was a murder mystery involving people who were well-liked and involved in the community. Not solving it weighed on the officers.

Chief Moore gave countless news interviews, and he credited the *Richmond County Daily Journal*, the *Charlotte Observer* and other newspapers for keeping the case in the headlines and helping keep attention on the deaths during the long investigation.

Bobbie Caldwell testified without any promise of immunity. After a nine-day trial, Joey Caldwell was found guilty on September 1, 1993. The next morning, he was found dead, hanging in his cell in the High Point Detention Center. He left notes for his family and for the jailers.

The day after the verdict, after Bobbie's involvement became public, she lost her job as a Mecklenburg County middle-school math teacher. She later pleaded guilty to conspiring to launder money and lying to a federal grand jury. She was sentenced to five years, the maximum penalty.

Outside the courtroom the day she was sentenced, Bobbie spoke briefly—for the first time—to Naomi Daggs, Maceo's girlfriend. "I have this deep sorrow I feel that won't go away," she said. "I think about you every day. I know what you lost."

GETTING AWAY WITH MURDER?

SMALL-TOWN LIFE

Rarely do suspected killers have the bravado to openly challenge investigators to "get on with it," so who can ignore a headline that reads: "Lincolnton Man Dares Officials to Charge Him in 1976 Killing"? The challenge was surprising enough. But that the death took place nineteen years earlier…in Pennsylvania, 650 miles away from North Carolina?

The story started—and ultimately ended—not in Charlotte but in Montrose, Pennsylvania, near Scranton. The Charlotte area, though, provided shelter and respite and new beginnings—as well as plenty of Charlotte headlines—during the decades-long saga.

The story started in 1971, when Martin Dillon, a twenty-five-year-old lawyer, met Dr. Stephen Scher, who was a few years older than Dillon, and the two men became buddies, even vacationing together with their wives.

Dillon and his wife, Patricia, had grown up in Montrose. Although she'd followed her mother's advice to become a nurse so she could marry a doctor, the family seemed pleased when she married the young lawyer. Marty, as he was called, was building his law practice mostly with bread-and-butter real estate closings, but he had also taken on his first murder defense. The couple had two small children.

Stephen Scher and his wife, Ann, had moved to Pennsylvania, where he began to specialize in treating allergies. He'd joined the Wednesday

Afternoon Club, a group of Marty Dillon's friends who took Wednesday afternoons off to go to Gunsmoke, the Dillon family's hunting retreat outside of town. Marty and Steve shot skeet and did regular "guy things" together… until late in the afternoon of June 2, 1976.

THE SCENE

That early June afternoon, Marty Dillon had tried to get the regular Wednesday group together for the trip to Gunsmoke, but other things pushed it off most of their schedules, leaving just Dillon and Stephen Scher driving to the camp in Dillon's BMW.

Dr. Scher said that after shooting several rounds, they'd returned to the trailer that served as Gunsmoke's base camp for more cigarettes. Scher had set his sixteen-gauge shotgun against a tree before going inside. Dillon spotted a porcupine, grabbed Scher's gun from where he'd propped it and gave chase into the woods. Scher heard the gun snap, he told the officer who took his statement at the scene. Then, a blast.

Eighteen years later, in a 1994 press conference reported by the *Charlotte Observer*, Scher remembered that he'd "yelled something like 'you couldn't hit the broad side of a barn.'…Then I saw him." His recounting of the story, over the years, had always included that hint of playful camaraderie between friends, the last bit of levity before the story turned dark.

Police notes recorded Scher's statement at the scene that afternoon: "I saw him lying on the ground face down. I ran up to him and turned him over and saw him bleeding from the chest. I tried to stop it but I couldn't. I gave him mouth to mouth but I knew he was dead." In a later statement, Scher said he tried to reach in through the wound and massage the heart. But his friend was gone.

Martin Dillon died of a shotgun blast to the chest.

News accounts at the time were too polite to report what the gossip around Montrose whispered—that Scher was having an affair with his best friend's wife, Patricia Dillon, a nurse he worked with at the hospital. As early as 1972, Montrose began flickering with tales of the doctor and nurse kissing in her driveway, him fondling her in front of other nurses, whispered heads-together conversations, rearranging their work schedules to work together and regular trysts behind locked doors at the hospital.

Scher was described by people who knew him as pushy, arrogant, plain-spoken or blunt, self-absorbed and someone who knew how to get what he wanted. But patients loved him. Patricia Dillon was described as stunning; even as the years passed, she was still the girl who'd worn a tiara to her high school prom even though she wasn't the prom queen.

Scher's wife, Ann, suspected an affair, but she also knew their marriage had begun deteriorating before any suspicions or rumors started.

Stephen Scher had filed for divorce in late 1975; Martin Dillon's law partner filed the papers for him. Scher denied any affair and went so far as to use his wife's accusations about an affair as a claim against her in his divorce petition.

Despite the gossip and drama, the coroner ruled thirty-year-old Martin Dillon's death an accident.

LIFE GOES ON

Only they could say how much the whispered rumors affected their decisions, but Dillon's widow and his best friend, Dr. Scher, both left Montrose and headed in opposite directions.

Pat Dillon took the two Dillon children and moved to Philadelphia. She learned that Martin had dropped her as his life insurance beneficiary, instead naming his two small children, so she worked to support them.

Stephen Scher had already been making plans to return to New Mexico, his home before he'd moved to Pennsylvania. He would practice medicine in Las Cruces, where he'd served on an Indian reservation early in his career.

The next official news came two years later, on June 18, 1978, when Patricia Dillon wed Stephen Scher in Las Cruces, New Mexico.

They were forced to explain their actions and their marriage years later, when the death investigation was reopened and the case again hit the headlines. Scher again denied they'd had an affair. He told reporters that he and Pat didn't start dating until two years after Dillon's death. Patricia told reporters that after they both left Montrose, Scher had been her only friend as she'd started a new life in Philadelphia. One day, late in 1977, Scher appeared at her door with a bag of groceries, and they began dating.

Curiously, his account of the dates doesn't quite fit her timeline, which claimed that they started dating two years after the death—yet they married two years and two weeks after the death? Of course, dates can get muddled in the midst of so much tragedy and new love.

SUSPICIONS

Martin Dillon's parents, Larry and Jo Dillon, weren't sending any happily-ever-after wishes. Larry Dillon continued to harbor deep suspicions about his son's death, and he had an intense focus on details that tragedy can sharpen. He'd heard the rumors about his daughter-in-law's affair. He wondered how his son had been killed with a number four shotgun shell when number eights are normally used for skeet shooting. When asked, Scher said he didn't know what was loaded in the gun—he just bought what was cheap.

Larry Dillon didn't think that explained anything, and he didn't believe his son was running with a shotgun shell racked in the chamber. Marty had been raised around guns; he had better sense.

Larry Dillon didn't know that others shared his suspicions.

One of the first responders to the scene at Gunsmoke, state trooper Frank Zanin, had suspicions from the day of the shooting, when he'd first spotted inconsistences between what he saw and what Scher said. Dillon's bootlace was untied, but the hunting boot was still snug against his leg; he couldn't have been running with it untied without the top of the boot working loose. The gunshot wound to Dillon's chest was too large for a contact wound, which would have left a small hole closer to the smaller diameter of the gun barrel. Zanin saw no blood spatter either inside or outside the shotgun barrel; "blowback" happens when a gun discharges close to the skin.

From the pattern of blood spatters and smears, Zanin could see that Dillon had been wearing his goggles and ear-protecting headset when the gun went off. Those small drops of blood and the streak where the ear protection was pulled off would become big evidence later.

Detective Jock Collier shared Zanin's suspicions about the inconsistencies, but cops are natively suspicious, while district attorneys and coroners have to deal with the political realities of cases. In small towns, those realities visit their offices and ballot boxes on a regular basis. Neither the district attorney nor the coroner believed that a doctor had gone out in the woods and shot a lawyer. They didn't see the evidence it would take to convince a jury otherwise.

So, the investigators filed away their paperwork, though Detective Jock Collier didn't consider it settled. He mailed Christmas cards to Las Cruces intended to unsettle Scher: "Thinking of you. Jock Collier."

Larry Dillon stewed. He and Collier kept in contact. He and his wife, Jo, prayed. Years went by. Larry was working a part-time job at a funeral home and was transporting a body to an autopsy when he happened to meet Zanin, the trooper who'd been first on the scene. Zanin told him the evidence was all still stored—the shotgun, Scher's clothing, Scher's initial statement, the photos.

NEW EVIDENCE

In November 1988, another piece of the puzzle found its place. Bonnie Mead had been Martin Dillon's secretary, had liked him, knew the rumors and had doubts about his death. In a new job at another firm, she worked on a civil case that involved an accident-reconstruction expert. After watching what Stewart Bennett, a former state trooper, had been able to do in their civil car accident case, she decided to just ask him her question out loud: Could you reconstruct what happened to Martin Dillon?

The former trooper knew the case and said he could. "I can't promise Larry Dillon it's going to be what he wants to hear," Bennett said. "But physical evidence doesn't lie. We can certainly tell what happened."

Pulling the necessary information from scattered sources took time, but in January 1990, Larry Dillon heard what he'd known all along: Bennett's tests showed that to make an entry wound that size, the gun barrel had to be three to five feet away—much too far for a self-inflicted wound caused by tripping. Martin Dillon couldn't have shot himself; it couldn't be an accident or suicide. This was homicide.

Larry Dillon had pushed law enforcement to get involved since Marty died. The scene reconstruction report was what Larry Dillon needed. Moving the wheels of any large bureaucracy takes time and tremendous effort, especially when asking state law enforcement officials to question the long-ago actions of local officials. But by May 1991, the Pennsylvania State Police and the FBI crime lab were looking at the case.

In 1992, the FBI lab reported a critical discovery: blood spatter and a small piece of Martin Dillon's tissue were found on Scher's boots and pants. This offered yet more proof of what Larry had suspected: Scher wasn't yards away; Scher was *right there* when the gun blast hit his son. Blood spatter—tiny droplets generated only by the velocity of a gunshot—can't appear after the fact from contact with a bleeding wound or blood drips. It occurs at the moment a high-velocity shot hits human tissue.

In 1994, to further nudge the slow wheels of bureaucracy and justice, Larry filed a civil lawsuit asking for the exhumation of his son's body and a second autopsy by a forensic anthropologist, one with the formal forensic training and experience that had been lacking during the first autopsy.

Patricia Scher and her two children—Martin's children, who had been raised by Stephen Scher after their dad's death—filed a countersuit opposing the exhumation. They didn't want his rest disturbed, and as his wife, she would typically decide what happened to his remains.

In a deposition—sworn testimony—given as part of Larry Dillon's lawsuit, Pat Scher was asked if she and Stephen Scher had been in love before Martin's death. "No," she said.

After being presented with evidence from both sides, the court ordered the exhumation.

Following the second autopsy, the new coroner's report agreed with the accident reconstruction. Martin Dillon's death was officially ruled a homicide, not an accident.

THE CASE

Once the Pennsylvania State Police got involved and the autopsy report was released, the investigation was deliberate and methodical. The prosecutor and investigators knew an old case would face challenges in front of a jury, and they wanted to make sure they had the evidence for not just an arrest but also a conviction.

In 1992 (coincidentally, the same year the FBI released the new lab results), the Schers left New Mexico and moved to Lincolnton, North Carolina (thirty-five miles northwest of Charlotte), to set up what became a thriving medical practice.

In 1994, only two years after the Schers settled in North Carolina, Pennsylvania state troopers showed up, knocking on doors in Lincolnton and continuing their investigation. They asked neighbors, colleagues and the hospital administrator about Scher. People were surprised by the questions and confused by any suspicions. One person told news reporter Chip Wilson: "I wondered why they [the investigators] spent the money to come down here," he said. "They aren't going to find anything wrong with him."

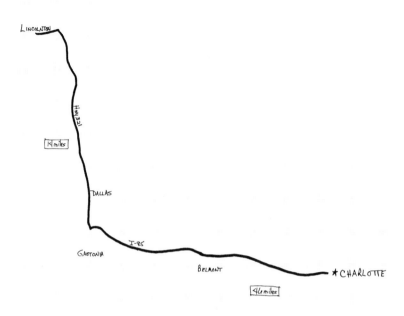

Map of the Lincolnton area. *Sketch by Cathy Pickens.*

THE NEWS CONFERENCE

The arrival of Pennsylvania investigators in Lincolnton and news about the autopsy results prompted the Schers to immediately pack their suitcases and drive ten hours to Scranton to the office of Scher's attorney. Eighteen years earlier, attorney Peter O'Malley had instructed Scher to not speak to the police about what happened at Gunsmoke. This time, they held a press conference in the attorney's office with O'Malley seated between the Schers.

In the press conference, Dr. Stephen Scher stuck with his original statements: he repeated the porcupine story he'd told after the death; he again denied any affair with Pat until well after Martin's death. The gist of his story didn't vary from the one he told so many years earlier, although he added some details, such as how he tried to massage his friend's heart and how they sometimes traded weapons because Dillon liked the lighter recoil on Scher's shotgun. He was also defiant: "Arrest me, and let's get on with it."

What the Schers didn't reveal to the press was that they'd driven to Pennsylvania expecting that Stephen would be arrested.

But he wasn't arrested—not then.

In 1995, the Pennsylvania attorney general took over the case, and Larry Dillon dropped his civil suit. The case was finally heading where Larry had always thought it should. The slow, methodical investigation continued. The North Carolina State Bureau of Investigation (SBI) and FBI agents didn't come for Scher until a year later, in Lincolnton, in June 1996.

The Trial

At the trial in September 1997, the twists in the case continued. Stephen Scher changed his story for the first time.

As *Charlotte Observer* columnist Tommy Tomlinson pointed out, the two children—Martin Dillon's children, who knew Scher as their loving dad—didn't get to hear the new version firsthand. They were outside the courtroom and not allowed to listen to testimony, because they themselves were scheduled to testify to support Scher. Larry and Jo Dillon, the children's grandparents, who now sat on the opposite side of the courtroom from their ex-daughter-in-law, did get to hear it firsthand from Scher's own mouth.

At the trial, faced with the damaging blood spatter and tissue forensic evidence from the FBI lab, Scher admitted that no porcupine had been present at the scene that day. He admitted Martin had confronted him about rumors of an affair. He had confessed to Martin that the rumors were true.

Martin asked him directly, and "I just had—I had to tell him the truth," Scher testified. "He was looking me in the eye. I could no longer keep it from him. I said, 'Yes, we're having, not a love affair, but a physical affair.' And then he became very anxious and very, very upset. He was sitting there on the log and he had his hand over his ears and he was rocking."

Scher said he was looking at the ground, embarrassed "to talk to him this way." He told Martin it was as much his (Martin's) fault as anybody's, referring to the long hours Martin worked building his law practice and how much he was away from Pat.

He heard Martin yell. He looked up. Martin had the gun. "I—I knew—I just knew I had to get that gun away. I had to get it. I didn't know what he was going to do with it. I just knew with his state of mind at that time and my state of mind that it wasn't good to have a hold of a gun and I lunged."

The gun fired. Scher said he never intended for his friend to die. It was an accident; it went off in the struggle.

It took twenty-one years for Scher to admit to the rumors and suspicions about the affair. The bag of groceries delivered to Pat's doorstep in Philadelphia had come earlier in their relationship than they'd admitted. Of course, people in Montrose already knew that. Small-town folks don't always stay home. Sometimes they visit big cities like Philadelphia—where someone saw Scher and Pat in the lingerie section of the iconic Wanamaker's department store. That story had circulated through town soon after Marty's death.

At trial, jurors also heard about the scene at Gunsmoke from Carol Gazda, a volunteer in first aid with the local ambulance squad. Her husband, who was also at the scene, had told her she wasn't needed in the woods and couldn't help. So, she sat in the car with her young daughter, waiting. At the car in front of hers was a man she didn't know. He "was just looking around, you know, normal. And then when someone came near to talk to him, he would get very emotional and start, you know…'My best friend is dead, I can't believe he's dead.'…When they left, he seemed fine again, like he was previous when he was alone. And when somebody came again, he'd do the same thing. It was kind of strange to me."

At trial, Scher admitted for the first time that he tried to stage the scene: he untied one of Dillon's shoelaces to make the story that he'd tripped more plausible. When a neighbor got to the scene, Scher smashed the shotgun into a tree in a fit and broke it. But why? To show how distraught he was, how angry he was at the gun? To destroy or confuse any evidence?

That Scher decided to change his story after so many years stunned the courtroom and those following the case in the Charlotte news. Robert Campolongo, the zealous prosecutor, had built his case without Scher's new version, but the changed story now allowed the prosecutor to add the label "liar"—by Scher's own admission—to his accusations against Scher.

In his testimony, Scher continued to say it was an accident. They were wrestling. The gun just went off. He didn't murder his friend.

The prosecutor, who had so meticulously gathered the evidence, pointed out the shattering fallacy in Scher's picture of what happened. The blood patterns on a tree stump at the scene said Dillon was crouched, as if loading the skeet machine. Clay target "pigeons" lay intact near his body. More importantly, the blood evidence showed that Dillon had been wearing the ear-protecting headset when he was shot. Smears on his head showed the headset was pulled off after he was shot. Why would he be wearing a headset if he and Scher were having this intense conversation about Dillon's wife?

On October 22, 1997, the jury ignored the options of lesser offenses, including involuntary manslaughter and homicide by misadventure, and found Scher guilty of the maximum offense: first-degree murder. The sentence was life without parole.

New Twists

At first, the prosecutor hadn't wanted to pile on charges after Pat Scher's second husband was convicted of murder, but he later decided he had no option but to charge her with perjury. The basis for the charge was her deposition in Larry Dillon's civil lawsuit. When questioned under oath, she denied being in love with Stephen Scher before Marty's death. Witnesses couldn't be allowed to lie.

A few months later, a judge dismissed the perjury charges against her, ruling she hadn't perjured herself because the attorney, chastely, hadn't asked her about sex—only about love. Sex and love aren't the same thing, the judge said. Based on that ruling, Pat Scher no longer faced felony charges. Two months later, she pleaded guilty to the remaining misdemeanor charge, "false swearing" for lying under oath, and was sentenced to a $500 fine, probation and community service.

The criminal sentences didn't end the twists for the Schers and the Dillons. In June 1999, after spending less than two years of his life sentence inside, Scher walked out of prison. The Pennsylvania Court of Appeals had reversed his conviction, ruling that the case should have been brought earlier and that the delay in prosecuting the case denied Scher his due process rights because witnesses had died and evidence was lost. He couldn't properly defend himself, all because the prosecutors didn't move faster to build their case against him.

The Commonwealth of Pennsylvania appealed the appellate court's ruling, but in the meantime, Scher was free.

He and Pat returned to Lincolnton; after a couple of years, they moved to a house in nearby Dallas, North Carolina. The Charlotte area continued to be home and haven for them, even though the North Carolina Medical Board refused to reinstate his license to practice medicine.

In 2002, more news hit: The Pennsylvania Supreme Court overruled the lower court and told Scher to come back to prison. The Schers' new neighbors in Dallas were surprised when they learned who he was. In the manner of neighbors being interviewed by reporters, they said they didn't know Scher well, but he was a nice guy.

Scher's lawyer flew from Pennsylvania, and the two spent the night in a Gastonia motel before catching a plane from Charlotte the next morning for Wilkes-Barre, where he turned himself over to state troopers.

In 2004, the court ordered a second trial, which created yet more upheaval and uncertainty for the families. In March 2008, after two hours of deliberation, another jury again convicted Stephen Scher, now age sixty-seven, of first-degree murder in the death of Martin Dillon. The automatic sentence was life without parole.

The Pennsylvania Supreme Court's opinion summed up a key element in the case: Why did it take so long for the investigators and prosecutors—at both the state and local levels—to get on the same page, to recognize what those first on the scene and jurors saw?

In the court's written opinion, Justice Sandra Schultz Newman acknowledged the role that small-town sensibilities played:

> *Perhaps, as Scher argues, those investigators should have been more circumspect in accepting his tale and pursued their suspicions more thoroughly, but we cannot find the Commonwealth's actions towards Scher so egregious when, in a small town, in a rural part of Pennsylvania with a part-time District Attorney, those responsible for enforcing the law would find it difficult to disbelieve the word of a respected physician. Nor can we ignore the benefit that Scher gained by lying to authorities rather than remaining silent: He enjoyed his liberty for twenty years.*

By the time of the second trial, Pat Scher had divorced the doctor. He died in prison in October 2010 at age seventy.

Stephen Scher had loyal friends and patients in New Mexico, Pennsylvania and North Carolina who believed in him to the very end and felt the punishment was too harsh—if any punishment was due at all. But Scher also faced a father who wasn't going to let his son die in the woods while his rival rode off with his son's widow and children—his grandchildren. Had Larry Dillon not spent years pushing for an investigation, the Schers could have stayed in their Lincolnton haven, enjoying life in their new small town.

Larry Dillon died before Scher was released for those few years, before the second trial was ordered. He and his wife, Jo, were estranged from their grandchildren despite how hard Jo had tried to stay in contact and be involved in their lives when they were young, before the trials. Marty Dillon's children remained loyal to their stepfather, the man who'd raised them, and who, based on the reports given, was a good dad. Larry and Jo Dillon felt the separation deeply. Prayer had sustained them as they sought justice and also in their losses.

Tragedies, especially those with the closeness common in families and in small towns, often end without clear answers, and "closure" rarely brings the hoped-for peace.

4

GANGS AND GANGSTERS

Charlotte began its days as a trading post and crossroads supporting the rural economy around it. Folks came to town to shop, to trade and, perhaps, to travel on to other places. Without the population density and flash of cities like New York, Chicago and Los Angeles, Charlotte maintained her quiet gentility, staying a relatively small city until the late twentieth century.

That doesn't mean Charlotte hasn't seen her share of big-city "organized" crime—some that flaunted her southern gentility, and some that had southern redneck flair.

HOMEGROWN BOOTLEGGING

Maybe Charlotte managed to avoid old-line gangster troubles because it maintained a steady flow of homegrown bootleg liquor throughout Prohibition—and beyond. After all, what's the point of being in the center of a rural farming region if you aren't surrounded by those who know how to grow corn and how to rig mechanical means for distilling spirits? The region had plenty of both.

The links between the region's stock car racing and bootlegging are well documented. When crop prices fell during the Depression, farmers in the southern Appalachian Mountains found that cooking corn liquor fit their

A view looking north on Tryon Street in 1925, during the bootlegging days. *Courtesy of Robinson-Spangler Carolina Room, Charlotte Mecklenburg Library.*

skill sets and generated more cash than other crops. Charlotte provided a lucrative sales outlet.

Even after the repeal of Prohibition, plenty of folks saw no reason to start paying taxes on their liquor manufacturing operations. Naturally, the federal revenue agents were on the lookout for those "running 'shine" down the twisting mountain roads, and the game was on. Junior Johnson, member of the NASCAR Hall of Fame, located in uptown Charlotte, has openly spoken about his early life running moonshine out of Wilkes County.

Charlotte has shared in other changing fashions of crime. Smuggling cigarettes became lucrative because North Carolina charged low state taxes on the end-product of its important tobacco crop. In 2003, Mohamad Hammoud from Lebanon was convicted of smuggling cigarettes from North Carolina to Michigan and using the profits from selling them in the higher-taxed states to provide funds for Hezbollah.

As was true in Chicago during Prohibition, as different waves of drugs washed into Charlotte over the years, different gangs fought for control of the market and the money. In the 1980s, crack, an altered and smokable form of cocaine, brought a drug popular among the rich to the street. Crack dealers were younger, more unpredictable and often more violent. Low-income sections of Charlotte became open-air drug markets; neighborhoods like Piedmont Courts, Dalton Village and Double Oaks were taken over by the Mustang Gang, the Posse, a young man called Money Rock and others.

More aggressive federal drug sentencing laws, more aggressive policing, a round-up of Mustang Gang members in 1992 and the 1995 conviction of the twenty-three-year-old man who cooked the rock for various gangs presaged not an end to but a definite lull in the crack epidemic's violent mark on the city. Tougher enforcement helped curtail the violence in those neighborhoods, but the same families who lived surrounded by gunfire were then faced with the loss of fathers, sons and brothers to the prison system. In her book *Money Rock*, former *Charlotte Observer* journalist Pam Kelley followed the story of one of Piedmont Court's flashiest young drug dealers from his early days to his successful post-prison life. While drugs and street gangs never completely disappear from any city, and the solutions are never easy, Kelley's account shows that individual stories of both loss and redemption lie behind those statistics.

THE CRUSADER

As the crackdown gained traction, one of Charlotte's healing influences from the fallout of the drug wars came in an unexpected package. The street gangs' legendary violence collided with the strength of religious faith in the story of Barbara Cameron, a woman who lost her husband to violence, studied and became an ordained minister and faced down gang members who took out a $3,000 hit on her life. She is credited with transforming one of the most crime-ridden neighborhoods in Charlotte.

In the Double Oaks neighborhood north of uptown, between Interstate 77 and Statesville Avenue, the sound of gunshots at night became common in the early 1970s. For Barbara Cameron, as with most residents, it was little more than background noise coming through the screen door until the day a neighbor came running with news that Barbara's husband, Casey Brewton, lay in the street.

He survived long enough at the hospital to tell her not to leave him. Then, he died, and her life was derailed. She left Charlotte and turned her back on what had become a deadly neighborhood until one day, God got ahold of her. She moved back to Charlotte and back to that neighborhood.

Charlotte Observer reporter Jeff Elder wrote about her remarkable journey and how Double Oaks (now the Genesis Park area) had been a good place to raise kids until drugs brought in money and violence and the kind of social decay associated with the word "gangs."

Cameron told Elder, "The squirrels wouldn't even come here. The shooting was so bad."

Her fight for the neighborhood was effective. Her work with children and police started threatening drug revenues and, perhaps more critically, the turf and status of gang leaders. A showdown was inevitable.

One day, gang members confronted her, flashing Uzis under their jackets. Her response was direct: "I'm going to give you a chance to find Jesus….And if you don't, buddy, you're going down."

Nobody talked to gun-toting gang members like that. They went looking for a hit man willing to work for a $3,000 bounty and found Michael Fitzsimmons out of Philadelphia. He knew his way around street violence; he looked to be the right man to take down the upstart preacher. When, years later, *Observer* columnist Kays Gary asked him how many people he'd killed, Fitzsimmons said, "Let's put it this way: I could take care of anything you needed done."

That was true until Fitzsimmons saw Coleman in action for himself and heard her preaching. "She's speaking God's truth," he said. She—and God—helped him turn his life around.

And she helped turn around the neighborhood with the highest rate of crime in Charlotte—and one of the most violent in the nation, according to the *New York Times*. Crime in the Genesis Park/Double Oaks neighborhood tumbled starting in 1989, and it continued to fall despite the crack-fueled crime increases in the early 1990s. Cameron started the Harvest Center in the 1980s as a feeding ministry; it is still in operation over thirty years later, offering housing, job training and other services along with community partners.

As for Michael Fitzsimmons, the hired gun, he spent time in prison for armed robbery but says Barbara Cameron changed his life. He told reporter Jeff Elder, "She's a beautiful, hard-working woman. She's like my second mom."

Crusading pastor Barbara Cameron died on December 5, 2008, while in her early sixties, but not before she proved that gang battles can have unexpected outcomes and unlikely gladiators.

THE OLDEST PROFESSION

Criminal enterprises don't have to involve large gangs; some keep it in a close circle. Sallie Wamsley (more commonly known as Sallie Saxon) ran her HushHush.com high-class prostitution ring with help from her husband, Donald Saxon, and a photographer friend, Glenn Fox. The smaller the circle, the easier to stay below police notice, she reasoned. Despite her careful precautions against getting caught, including detailed background checks on customers, she was indicted in 2007.

The HushHush.com website advertised "the Finest in Southern Hospitality" and "nonsexual companionship only" for an $1,800 membership fee. The *Charlotte Observer* called it "one of the most sophisticated internet-based prostitution rings in the country." Part of the city's fascination with the case was that a woman operated it out of a suburban ranch house in the McClintock Woods neighborhood off Rama Road. Sallie Saxon booked hotel rooms using Priceline; accepted major credit cards, PayPal and prepaid gift cards; and kept meticulous records dating back years (which had to cause concern with her clients once the story broke).

When the *Observer* began reporting details from the unsealed court documents, people around town started trying to figure out whose names matched her clients' initials and marveled at the monies paid for services (up to $700 an hour). The sex workers reportedly kept 70 percent of the fees, and Saxon did background checks on both her clients and her workers—but the precautions weren't enough. Her company was incorporated in 1997; the FBI, IRS and local police started investigating her in 2000.

In 2008, after agreeing to turn over her business records and client list, Sallie was sentenced to two years in federal custody and forfeited property and money. Donald Saxon and Glenn Fox got twenty-one-month and fifteen-month sentences, respectively. Some of Sallie's clients were prosecuted and pleaded guilty.

This wasn't the only prostitution ring busted in Charlotte and operated by a respectable-looking businessperson. In the 1990s, Darryl Pruitt had controlling interest of much of Charlotte's prostitution business, with at least thirty-five escort services charging around $125 an hour. In 1995, such businesses advertised in the Southern Bell Yellow Pages, not online. Using aliases, Pruitt would obtain business licenses and phone lines, take out ads and then lease the numbers to smaller entrepreneurs.

In July 1995, a couple of years before Saxon incorporated HushHush, a federal grand jury indicted forty-three-year-old Pruitt and his companion,

Erica Lynn Norton, age twenty-seven, for money laundering and conspiracy to aid racketeering. At the time, Pruitt gave a Chesterfield Avenue house as his business address, but he also owned a home on Lake Wylie and a condo on Carmel Road.

Peace and Love

In addition to drugs and prostitution, Charlotte also had its counterculture "gang." The Red Hornet May Day Tribe made headlines for burning a U.S. flag and for the lawsuit they filed after they were turned away from the Billy Graham Day celebration at the original coliseum on Independence Boulevard. In October 1972, President Richard Nixon attended the celebration to honor native son Billy Graham, and the tribe saw an opportunity to protest Nixon's war policies. In a court hearing on their case, the judge allowed them to sing, with the musical accompaniment of a kazoo, the song they'd planned to perform for Nixon about "land of the freaks and home of the grave."

The "long-hairs," as they were identified in news reports, also had signed a warrant for assault against Dr. Graham's wife, Ruth, for pushing one of their members, taking his sign, sitting with it under her feet and not giving it back.

The tribe lost its federal civil lawsuit.

The Red Hornet May Day Tribe became famous not only for causing trouble but for being the target of trouble from an unexpected direction. The tribe, described by Ann Wicker in *Creative Loafing* as including "members of Charlotte's own leftwing hippie commune," was part of a collective that ran Crazy Horse Books uptown on Sixth Street. Longtime residents remember when City Fair was built there, across from the main library; the Hearst Tower now dominates the skyline on that end of town. But in 1972, the counterculture bookshop on that block became the target of vandals who shot into the shop's windows.

The night after the store windows were damaged, two tribe members stayed in the store to keep watch. The pellet gun–wielding miscreants turned out to be three Charlotte police officers. As they drove off, the two police cars had easy-to-see identifying numbers. The officers were suspended, and the shop continued to operate for a while longer—windows intact.

THE ANGELS' FUNERAL

Charlotte's most iconic gangs have to be those who ride motorcycles. A rough-and-ready redneck edge, a simple directness to their violent drugs-and-prostitution business model, their beer bellies and shaggy beards—all seemed to be bespoke southern.

In the 1970s and 1980s, Charlotte was one of few cities to host chapters of several motorcycle gangs ("MCs," or motorcycle clubs, to those in the know): Hell's Angels, the Outlaws and the Pagans, as well as homegrown clubs like the Brothers, the Southern Gentlemen, Ghost Riders, the Knights, the Tasmanian Devils and the Tar Heel Stompers. The Stompers, in particular, developed a reputation for viciousness that rivaled any of the others, but they were known more to law enforcement than to the media, so little mention of them remains.

Thanks to books and movies and its national reach, the Hell's Angels came to symbolize both the allure and the treachery of biker gangs.

The Hell's Angels chapter in Charlotte was chartered on October 19, 1978, a few years after the South's first chapters were established in Charleston, South Carolina (February 7, 1976), and Durham, North Carolina (July 24, 1973). According to Yves Lavigne, Canadian journalist and chronicler of the Angels, Michael "Thunder" Finazzo, a charter member of the Omaha chapter dating from 1966, was sent with a couple of others to set up in Charlotte.

Finazzo was a member of the national club's Filthy Few, and he grew Charlotte's chapter into one of the most powerful in the country. The Filthy Few were the hard-partiers, the ones counted on to organize and carry out business, whether it was setting up a party or a hit. Many earned their distinctions by killing for the club.

Other motorcycle clubs already existed in the Charlotte area and controlled the drugs and prostitution. With determined violence, Finazzo and his right-hand man, Tyler Duris "Yank" Frndak, took over the Tar Heel Stompers and "turfed out" its president, Johnny Edsel High. Smaller regional clubs were subsumed into the Angels and the Outlaws until only the two larger clubs were left poaching each other's members and turf. Charlotte was one of the few cities in the country where both the Hell's Angels and the Outlaws operated, and turf battles were common.

Even if they couldn't ignore the X-rated stores on Wilkinson Boulevard that greeted visitors to the Charlotte-Douglas Airport, most people could ignore the violence the gangs brought, because it didn't affect them.

In September 1981, Charlotte club president Finazzo and Frndak were found stuffed in the trunk of a new, blue Oldsmobile 88. Yves Lavigne said their heads were wrapped in plastic to contain the blood, but apparently, that didn't work. Police investigated the car after a passerby reported blood dripping from the trunk. The Olds belonged to Finazzo's girlfriend, but police ruled out her involvement.

According to Lavigne, Finazzo became too powerful, and someone inside the Angels organization was sent to execute him. Finazzo refused to kneel for his execution, so they broke his leg and shot him in the back of the head.

For police, the case remains unsolved. Police believe the two were killed in Durham and were possibly being transported back to Charlotte when, for unknown reasons, they were left on a gravel road in Randolph County just outside Ramseur. With an abundance of subtlety, State Bureau of Investigation special agent in charge Scott Williams said, "As with most motorcycle gang investigations, the witnesses and suspects are generally not cooperative with law enforcement."

In keeping with club culture, on October 1, 1981, Hell's Angels from all over the United States—as well as England, the Netherlands, Denmark and Canada—came to Marshville, a small town about thirty-five miles from Charlotte, for the burial. The Angels had moved their Charlotte headquarters to a brick house on White Street in Marshville a year earlier. According to the town florist, the bikers ordered more flowers than the florist usually handled for Mother's Day and Christmas combined.

Marshville residents who lined the street to watch the procession were bemused, respectful and tolerant. One said, "I guess this is about the biggest thing that's ever happened in Marshville."

Reverend Paul McCartin, a motorcycle-riding priest at Our Lady of Lourdes Catholic Church in Monroe, was surprised when he was asked to officiate at the graveside service. He figured it was the motorcycle connection, but whatever the reason, he wasn't going to say no to a mother who had to bury her son. Mrs. Finazzo had traveled from Omaha. When he was a boy, Finazzo had regularly attended Mass and wanted to become a priest.

The event provided a window into a violent but colorful subculture. The *Charlotte Observer* ran multipage articles with photos of a double line of bikes stretched out behind the hearse and another of a tall, bearded bike club member waiting on the sidewalk, holding a drink cup as he propped one hand on a storefront and talked with a couple of curious Marshville residents. Representatives from rival clubs also came to pay their respects, including some Rebel Rousers from High Point.

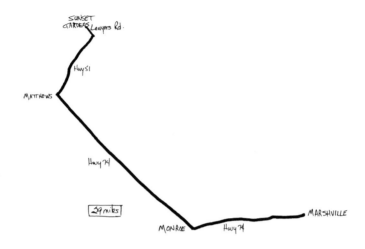

Map of funeral procession route from Marshville to Mint Hill cemetery. *Sketch by Cathy Pickens.*

Motorcycle funeral procession from Marshville to Mint Hill. *Courtesy of* Charlotte Observer *and Charlotte Mecklenburg Library.*

International Hell's Angels members attending the funeral for Michael "Thunder" Finazzo and Tyler Frndak. *Courtesy of* Charlotte Observer *and Charlotte Mecklenburg Library.*

Left: Michael Finazzo's headstone in Mint Hill cemetery. *Photo by Cathy Pickens.*

Right: Hell's Angels medallion at gravesite. *Photo by Cathy Pickens.*

Investigators noted their appearance with interest, given rumors that the Rousers, who'd been known as Hell's Angels associates, had been meeting with the Outlaws.

The funeral procession moved from the Marshville funeral home to Sunset Memory Gardens near Mint Hill, the venue for the burial of Terry Surrat, an Outlaws member, in 1975. Finazzo and Frndak were buried side by side. Artie Cherry, another member of the Filthy Few, joined them in the plot a year later, in 1982.

Only fellow club members are allowed to "throw dirt" or cover the casket of another member.

IN OTHER BIKER NEWS

Until the lengthy coverage of the funeral, local news coverage of biker activity was usually pithy. One such notice appeared in the *Observer* on July 27, 1979, in so few lines that many readers would overlook it. Only years later would the public learn the story behind the tiny news item:

> *Murder Charge: Mecklenburg County police have charged a Charlotte man with killing another man in a fight Dec. 16. Gregory Scott "Angel" Lindaman, 23, of 2214 N. Brevard St. was arrested Tuesday in California on a Charlotte warrant in a motorcycle theft. After he was returned to Charlotte, Lindaman was charged with murdering Larry "Popeye" Pressley, a former member of the Tarheel Stompers motorcycle gang. Pressley was killed in the parking lot at Trader Don's Lounge on the Mount Holly–Huntersville Road. Lindaman is believed to have been a member of the Outlaws motorcycle gang.*

That's not the kind of news most Charlotte readers would notice; it was just another example of why they didn't have to worry about the bikers—they beat and killed each other, not random citizens.

Two years before the 1981 Hell's Angel's headlining funeral and three weeks before the tiny article about Angel Lindaman, another biker killing featured in a story that would claim headlines for over thirty years: the July 4, 1979 massacre at the Outlaws clubhouse. The story had shock value, even if those involved weren't folks most Charlotteans would meet at work or in church or at the mall.

Shock No. 1: Five people were shot to death on a quiet, blue-collar street in a dingy house at 2500 Allen Road South.

Shock No. 2: One or two killers came in and quickly and effectively shot members of a notoriously tough motorcycle gang; no one fired a defensive shot or landed a blow.

Shock No. 3: This was the most stunning news—one of the victims was a seventeen-year-old girl whose mama kept hoping she'd come to her senses, leave the biker life and come home to Gastonia. As each anniversary passed, the newspaper ran her smiling school photo. Five-foot-tall Bridgette "Midget" Benfield could have been anybody's kid or sister or neighbor. She'd been asleep on the sofa, her head on a biker's shoulder.

The investigation was thorough. No one wanted a gang war in town, and this had all the makings. But in the closed world of gang culture, no one talks. Or, as Yves Lavigne reported, the Hell's Angels motto was: "Three can keep a secret if two are dead."

Someone kept the secret for almost forty years.

The break in many cold cases—not just biker cases—comes after the major players are dead. Those who've held their silence for decades usually have good reasons for doing so. Fear of reprisal would have topped the list.

The July 4 massacre remained among Charlotte's worst unsolved murders until the day that small news article about the biker brought back to town in 1979 took on new meaning.

The police had suspected the real culprits almost from the start, but they hadn't been able to make a case. As with so much that hits the headlines, much more happens behind the scenes but is not quite ready to be reported, fleshed out or finished. Only after enough time had passed was the story ready to be told.

In 2015, an informant gave police two names: Gregory Scott "Angel" or "Teen Angel" Lindaman and Randy Allen Pigg. The two had been on the periphery of the Outlaws, but not members. One of them had a grudge to settle with someone in the clubhouse. They knew enough about the club's workings that they knew when and how to strike. The other four victims were collateral damage.

The police admitted that closing a case after the killers were dead was less than satisfying. Lindaman died in Houston in 1990 doing what was described as a "Batman turn" in his Corvette. Pigg died of liver disease in hospice care in 2007.

The case stayed in Charlotte's collective memory not because burly bikers fought with and killed each other but because, over the course of thirty-six years and four days, the smiling school photo of a young Midget Benfield appeared in anniversary news articles about the cold case.

To say that technology took down the violent motorcycle gangs would be simplistic—but not inaccurate. Police infiltration of the clubs on the national level and a local crackdown on adult bookstores made inroads into the biker gangs' lucrative business model. But the advent of internet porn and prostitution's shift to online solicitation also cut into their business. The gang lifestyle wasn't one that promised longevity, either. Thunder Finazzo was forty when he was shot; Yank Frndak was thirty. Those killed at the Outlaws headquarters in 1979 ranged in age from seventeen to thirty-two.

THE WOMAN WHO LOVED HORSES

Easter Weekend

Around 4:00 a.m. on the Saturday of Easter weekend, March 29, 1997, a red Jeep Wrangler was found at the side of Old Charlotte Highway outside Monroe with the engine running, the headlights on and the driver's window down, as if the driver had just stepped away.

By Easter Sunday afternoon, as word spread that a local woman was missing under odd circumstances, friends and family and people who didn't know her spread out to search, hoping to find her.

One Monroe man had a premonition and decided the Westwood Industrial area was a logical place to look—it was wooded and not far from where her Jeep was found, but little traveled.

His premonition proved accurate. He and a friend found her body in the tree-sheltered lovers' lane, hidden under leaves, roofing shingles, branches and a wooden pallet, less than two miles from her Jeep on a dead-end road near Monroe Airport and Westwood Industrial Drive.

At her funeral, held the following Thursday at Mount Carmel United Methodist Church, the crowd was so large that some mourners had to sit outside.

An Easter weekend shouldn't end that way. Kim Medlin dreamed of owning her own horse farm, and she worked two jobs to make that happen. Her day job at the Monroe Livestock Auction reflected her love of horses and

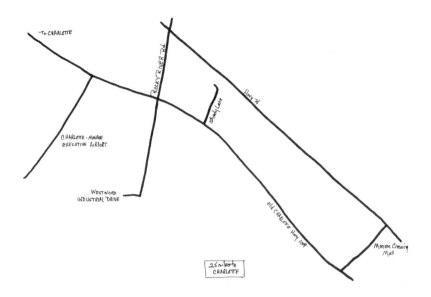

Map of the Monroe area. *Sketch by Cathy Pickens.*

Memorial at the site where the body was discovered. *Courtesy of* Charlotte Observer *and* Charlotte Mecklenburg Library.

drew little comment, but news reports were quick to mention her other job as a waitress at The Men's Club in Charlotte. Though her waitress uniform was a full bodysuit topped with a dress jacket, the edginess of working in a strip club was the kind of detail that captured attention. To Kim, it was nothing more than a second job—a way to save toward her dream.

Family photos show a beautiful blonde with hair swinging down her back, looking outdoorsy and energetic even in still photos. She and Bridger Medlin seemed one of those storybook young couples—attractive, with dreams of a future, working hard to make those dreams come true. They lived close to family and enjoyed each other's company.

Bridger worked as a disc jockey, but his family had farmed, and he said Kim "brought me back to that." They'd already built her horse barn.

Bridger was tall and handsome, with flowing blond hair, a distinctive handlebar mustache and an ease with cameras and in interviews that kept the case in the spotlight during the two months of investigation. But his willingness to talk also drew some suspicion. "Look at the husband first," a lot of amateur detectives said, with raised eyebrows.

Kim and Bridger had a slow courtship. He met her at one of her waitressing jobs, and they'd been friends for a while before they started dating. One night, Bridger said, they were slow-dancing at the Holiday Inn on Woodlawn in Charlotte when Kim pointed out it was their fifth date and he still hadn't kissed her. They married in September 1994.

THE COMMUTE

The drive between her night job and her home south of Monroe was less than an hour. Old Charlotte Highway had traffic even at 3:00 a.m. As she customarily did, she called Bridger from her car phone to tell him she was on her way and would be home in about fifteen minutes.

Bridger, tired from DJing a prom in Manning, South Carolina, and driving home that night, fell asleep waiting. He started awake later, realizing she wasn't home. He called her car phone and was surprised when a man answered—a police officer at the scene. "Bridger, we found Kim's Jeep."

He rushed to the scene on Old Charlotte Highway and Shady Lane. A closed-circuit camera recorded his distinctive truck as it barreled through Monroe. He knew something was terribly wrong. Kim wouldn't stop for just anybody. She was cautious and smart. She would have fought, Bridger knew that.

Two weeks earlier, Kim had been harassed on her way home by two guys who had pulled up behind her, tailgating her, flashing their headlights and trying to run her off the road, seemingly angry with her. The incident shook her, and she pulled over as soon as she saw two Monroe city police cars parked together to report what happened.

After she drove toward home, the two officers searched the nearby area. They found the car she described down the street. The driver thought she'd driven up behind them with her lights on bright, deliberately blinding them. The officers decided it was all a misunderstanding, but a BOLO (be on the lookout) was broadcast to all officers so they could keep an eye out for her on the nights she routinely drove home late.

Had her disappearance been a continuation of that road rage? Had someone targeted her, finding her again on her way home from work? Or had someone followed her from the club, waiting until she got to a remote area?

THE SUSPICIONS

As word spread around Charlotte and Monroe on Sunday that a beautiful young blonde was missing, rumors sprouted, sparked by the nature of her work and only compounding her family's grief.

One officer believed he'd seen Bridger in town that night at the time when he'd said he was home. But police quickly cleared him from their suspect list thanks to closed-circuit television recordings from area businesses and cell tower records. Bridger's truck was not seen on surveillance video until after he learned her Jeep had been found. His cell phone pings confirmed he'd been home, where he said he was, not roaming downtown Monroe or the Old Charlotte Highway.

Bridger certainly felt the public and private questions. Someone told him during the investigation that in 95 percent of the cases when something happens to a wife or girlfriend, the guy in her life is involved. Bridger Medlin's parents even got phone calls the afternoon they returned home from the funeral asking if it was true that Bridger had confessed to killing her.

Amid the rumors, the police were busy but quiet. They held details close, not revealing how she died or what they thought happened as she

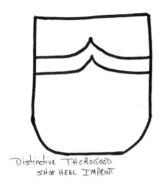

Distinctive THOROGOOD
SHOE HEEL IMPRINT

Sketch of the distinctive
Thorogood heelprint—key
evidence in the case. *Sketch by
Cathy Pickens.*

drove home in the dark morning hours. They wouldn't even confirm that her purse was still on the Jeep's seat, missing only her driver's license, though her family openly shared that with the press.

Neither police nor the public ignored the open driver's-side window and missing license. Bridger insisted she'd only stop for a police officer, but there had been no police call-in for a stop on her Jeep that night. The next logical fear was a blue-light bandit—a predator posing as a police officer.

Coincidentally, Charlotte police were investigating two separate blue-light bandits operating at that time. One, as it turned out, had recently been arrested, but the second was still unidentified. Victims said he would try to solicit them after pulling them over, so he remained an open avenue.

The autopsy provided other investigative leads. State Bureau of Investigation (SBI) latent print analyst Rick Navarro found a shoe imprint with a distinctive chevron-patterned heel on the back of her sweatshirt. He sifted through exemplars and identified only one with that distinctive heel tread: a Thorogood Clarino shoe, men's size eight, eight and a half or nine.

Only one store in Monroe sold that type of shoe, and the store sold them to only one customer: Monroe Public Safety, the police department.

Only three officers in the one-hundred-and-ten-member force wore shoes in that size range; one of them was Roger Griffin, who'd been one of the two officers Kim approached two weeks earlier when she was frightened by a tailgater on her way home. He was eliminated as a suspect—the night of her murder, he was on duty at the firehouse with plenty of witnesses. The second officer was accounted for on other calls, also with witnesses. The third officer was Josh Griffin, Roger's son.

Josh lived with his mom and his twin brother. People described Josh as the stereotypical boy next door and "one of the sweetest boys you've ever seen." He had long dreamed of being a police officer. He'd trained in Central Piedmont Community College's program (at his own expense rather than waiting for a department to hire him and pay the tuition), then was hired as a jailer with the Union County Sheriff's Office in Monroe in May 1995. He moved to a patrol officer position with Monroe police five months later.

Josh Griffin. *Courtesy of* Charlotte Observer *and Charlotte Mecklenburg Library.*

Like a lot of officers, he also worked a second security job for the extra money; his was at Monroe Mall.

That's where he was until 10:30 p.m. on the Friday before Easter, providing security at the mall on Independence Boulevard, the main road between Charlotte and Monroe. As was allowed in Monroe (and other jurisdictions), he wore his Monroe officer's uniform and drove his patrol car on his security job.

After work, he said he'd been sitting in his car near Old Charlotte Highway and Rocky River Road for about an hour after his shift ended reading a law book. During that time, he pulled two young females and a man for minor driving violations; he gave them verbal warnings but didn't call any of them in to dispatch.

Around 2:00 a.m., a man came to Josh's parked car asking for help getting his car out of a nearby ditch; again, Josh didn't use his radio but instead called a wrecker on his personal phone.

Josh said he got home about 2:30 in the morning.

The evidence said that wasn't true.

THE INVESTIGATION

On May 28, 1997, two months after Kim was found, news reports of the autopsy findings were released: multiple scrapes and injuries to her face and head, a fracture at the base of her skull and a fractured hyoid bone—an indication of strangulation. A spent shotgun shell was tangled in her hair. She was not sexually assaulted.

Three days after the autopsy findings were released, headlines confirmed what had been widely speculated when a Monroe police officer was charged with murder.

Rookie Monroe public safety officer Josh Griffin, age twenty-four, was arrested, booked and held in protective custody in the Mecklenburg

County Jail for his own safety because he had worked in the Union County jail in Monroe not many months before his arrest. His booking photo shows a good-looking young man with blond hair, a square jaw and blue eyes.

This was no "blue-light bandit" with a mail-order roof light pretending to be a police officer in order to waylay women on lonely roads. This was a real police officer, with his city-issued uniform, city patrol car and regulation black Thorogood uniform shoes.

What had not been publicized during the investigation—though rumors had sprouted quickly—was that Josh came under suspicion as early as April 7, barely a week after Kim's body was found. He'd been seen driving his patrol car that night after he was supposed to be off duty. A friend said Josh loved police work so much that he often drove extra patrols after his shift. Josh said he sometimes couldn't sleep at night after his shift ended, so he'd just stay out.

On April 11, after North Carolina State Bureau of Investigation agents searched Josh's home, the police chief confirmed to reporters that Griffin was under investigation.

Griffin's patrol car was searched. The chief said it was unexpectedly clean—Josh was known for having one of the messiest cars in the squad. Despite the cleaning, the SBI found human blood and light-colored hair in the car.

Few investigative details made it into the local newspapers or television coverage. The chief didn't publicly confirm the missing driver's license. He didn't talk about the shoe impression that matched the size and tread of Josh's uniform shoe; that information officially became public knowledge at the trial.

The police kept mum about what they were doing, what they were finding and what they suspected. As a result, those following the case assumed they weren't doing enough. After all, this was a small-town police force. What could they know?

That raised other complaints as the case unfolded and tidbits emerged and were dissected over coffee or at the water cooler. The *Charlotte Observer* reported that Monroe citizens were concerned that off-duty officers were allowed to wear their uniforms and drive their patrol cars while moonlighting. Most communities like having officers as visible as possible in neighborhoods and at businesses. Now that those emblems of authority had helped commit a murder, any perceived benefits vanished from the public's mind, replaced by questions.

Citizens also complained that Monroe officers stayed involved with the investigation even though one of their own was a "person of interest." They didn't know or didn't think it provided sufficient separation when the State Bureau of Investigation joined the case as soon as suspicions about Josh arose.

As is common when violence hits close to home in a normally peaceful community, citizens also wanted to know why it took two long months to arrest him. Gathering evidence and waiting on test results can never happen as quickly as it does on television. Failing to take enough time to meticulously build a case can make the difference between sending the right man to jail or setting the real killer free. But those explanations were too rational to subdue the specters raised by what Josh had done.

Mostly, citizens were stunned and saddened, first by the murder and then by the killer's identity.

Charlotte Observer columnist Dannye Romine Powell wrote about her poignant interview with Bridger in June 1997, about his awareness of "the great irony in this story":

> *"Kim died because she obeyed the law," he says. "This is the most unfair and betraying thing I can imagine. She would never speed. She would never drive without her seat belt. And she was pulled over.*
>
> *"Think about it," he says. "Here was a girl good as gold. She was working hard for her future, and she is dead.*
>
> *"And here is a man we put in the highest position of trust, and he's being charged with murder.*
>
> *"This is a major, major irony."*

THE TRIAL

At the end of July, Union County prosecutors announced they would seek the death penalty.

The trial was moved from Union County to Rowan County after the court searched for a county that had courtroom space for such a lengthy, high-profile trial with such strong ties—on both sides—within Union County.

At trial, the details of the story were presented to the public for the first time. Jurors and court watchers learned that Monroe officers used CB radios to talk "offline" between patrol cars. They heard that Josh Griffin "called another officer's attention to the 'babe' in the red Jeep…that he was going to get her license tag number, that defendant frequently engaged in the practice of 'running' the license tag numbers of attractive females to obtain personal information about them."

At first, during the investigation, Josh denied stopping her that night. He'd never called in the stop. But when investigators found physical evidence she'd been in his car, he admitted he'd pulled her over, admitted he'd put her in his car.

The jury had to draw what happened next from the circumstances, because Josh never admitted to anything that happened after the stop. She'd clearly been moved from the well-traveled highway to a desolate cul-de-sac. At some point, her wrists had been restrained. She'd been choked by something hard held against her windpipe. Maybe a police baton? A small bone in her neck was crushed.

After the two-month trial, jurors deliberated for five hours, finding Josh Griffin guilty of first-degree murder and first-degree kidnapping. When it came to the sentencing phase, only four jurors reportedly supported a death sentence in their first vote. They settled on a sentence of life in prison. Afterward, jurors were open about their sympathies for the pain felt by both families.

Investigators never found the shoes they knew Josh owned, with the distinctive chevron. He said they'd been ruined by battery acid at an accident scene, and he'd thrown them away. But as with much of the case, Josh had more than one version.

In 2005, while he was in prison serving his sentence, Josh admitted to an SBI investigator that the shoeprint was his. Afterward, he'd thrown the shoes in a commercial trash bin. He'd cut up Kim's driver's license and flushed it.

He also claimed he'd killed her at the behest of drug dealers who were holding them both at gunpoint. He owed the dealers money for steroids. The only lead he offered investigators was a very un-cop-like description: the drug dealers were "ordinary" and "average" in appearance. He didn't offer a plausible explanation as to why drug dealers had him waylay and kill Kim Medlin—or why he came up with that creative version of the facts so many years later.

Motorists—and women driving alone, in particular—are now routinely warned not to pull over in dark, lonely spots, not for anyone. Even if it appears to be a police officer, they should acknowledge the officer with their warning flashers and drive to a well-lit area with other people around before stopping.

Years of reports from all over the country have earned "blue-light bandit" a spot in the dictionary. Few places have been immune. Fortunately, though, there's no new dictionary term for a crime that causes people to reassess who they trust. Fortunately, such cases are rare.

THE DOCTOR AND THE HANDYMAN

CHARLOTTE NEWCOMERS

The case was ready-made to capture headlines: a young woman who'd longed to be a mother, supposedly safe in her own home on a lovely street in the Cotswold neighborhood with her newly adopted baby, found dead by her doctor husband when he came home from work late on July 27, 1990.

If the facts hadn't captured our imagination, Kim Thomas's photo would: dark, pixieish curls framing a face full of energy. She was small and slender, gathered friends easily and loved parties. She liked standing out, and according to her sister, she and her husband, Ed Friedland, loved "being the New Yorkers in town" when they moved to Charlotte.

Their long courtship started during their college years in Rochester, New York, then his hospital training in New York City. She followed him to Miami and, as a stockbroker (but without any broadcast experience), she'd been hired for an on-air financial analyst job with the local affiliate of the Financial News Network.

After she married her kidney-specialist husband in Miami, she moved with him to Charlotte in 1986, when he was hired as director for a dialysis center.

As Ed worked to build his Charlotte practice, Kim helped him with necessary start-up tasks like cleaning the office and bookkeeping. Later, to fill her time, she took a leadership role with the local chapter of the National

Police car parked on Wendover Road with the Friedland/Thomas house visible through the trees. *Courtesy of* Charlotte Observer *and Charlotte Mecklenburg Library.*

Organization of Women (NOW), earning her the sobriquet "activist." With a friend, she wrote *A Charlotte Child: A Guide for the Pregnant Woman*.

She and Ed bought a home full of windows and light on a deep, wooded lot just off Wendover Road. Those who knew her talked about her excitement over their newly adopted son. She'd always wanted a baby, and they were the first in North Carolina to have an independent adoption without using an agency.

Life looked good—until the evening her husband found her murdered on their dining room floor with her hands handcuffed behind her, her throat slashed multiple times and her ten-month-old baby crying in his crib.

In most family stories, when outsiders start poking around, looking too closely and asking questions, the cracks began to appear in even the happiest marriages. The common wisdom says to always look first at a husband or boyfriend; this husband could be distant and aloof, and he had affairs. When a call to Crimestoppers reported his affair at the time of the killing, that news and his attitude raised suspicions among the investigators in the first days of the case. The public, who followed the case unfolding in newspaper stories, also wondered. Ed wasn't coming across well in the glare of the publicity.

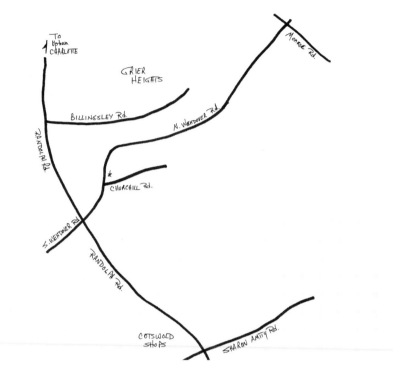

Map of the Wendover and Grier Heights area. *Sketch by Cathy Pickens.*

Kim's journals revealed how they'd gone back and forth for years about getting married. Before they married, she wrote to a friend that she didn't know if their marriage would work, but she could always get a divorce. In her journal, she detailed the difficulty of not being able to have a child and about Ed's distance. She wrote that Ed wasn't sure about them having a baby: "He thought we weren't stable enough to have a kid." He told her he wouldn't be around much; he would be working. She also wrote about how he made her laugh; she tended to fret, and he could turn stress into laughter. She said he was brilliant, graduating from Columbia University at age twenty.

She told her sister that they might be heading toward a divorce, but "I'm no fool. If we get divorced, I want to make sure that I am taken care of." But she also wrote, after the baby came, about how happy she was. She finally had the sense of family she'd longed for.

In short, the Thomas/Friedland marriage, like many relationships in their early stages, had its dreams and realities, its negotiations, its hurts and its happiness. But few relationships end with a mother murdered where she should have felt safe.

THE INVESTIGATION

When cases linger too long without an arrest, accusations that the police are sloppy or aren't paying attention often arise. According to *Charlotte Observer* reporter Elizabeth Leland, this was Charlotte's fifty-fourth homicide in 1990; by the end of the year, the total would be one of the high-water marks for Charlotte homicides: ninety-seven. At the time of Kim Thomas's murder, in 1990, the police department had only eight homicide investigators; by 1997 (when the murder rate was sixty-three, and all the cases that year were cleared), the department had twenty-two.

For neighborhood canvassing and following up on leads, the police pulled in officers from other assignments to help the homicide detectives; the organization of the information coming in tended to be somewhat haphazard. They had a lot happening with the investigation, a lot of other murders that year and too few experienced detectives.

Cases without new revelations eventually fall from the front page, sifting farther into the paper and claiming fewer and fewer column inches, until the story disappears. In the first year, when the case seemed to languish,

Officers brought in to canvas the neighborhood. *Courtesy of* Charlotte Observer *and Charlotte Mecklenburg Library.*

Kim's parents went public, asking for any information—the kind of work families do to keep a case in the public eye (and heart). Articles, always with her familiar photos, appeared on anniversaries; these were written to remind those who might have some information that it would be a kindness to share it.

For the family, do headlines remind them of the pain? Or do resurrections of the story remind them that others still care and give them hope that something new may surface?

Four years passed before the next breaking-news headline: in July 1994, Dr. Ed Friedland was formally charged with his wife's murder. Armchair detectives around town had been waiting for this, assuming he'd done it given the common wisdom about a cheating husband.

The judge granted Friedland bond, allowing him to return to his home rather than wait in jail for the trial.

In March 1995, in a pretrial hearing, Dr. Michael Baden, former New York City Medical Examiner and one of the star-power names in the forensic pathology world, appeared in a Charlotte court testifying as to the time of Kim's death. This was a key element of the case, because Friedland said he'd left about 7:45 or 8:00 that morning to go to work; coworkers corroborated when he arrived at the office. If she died before 7:30, he was there when she died. If she died later, he couldn't have done it.

Mecklenburg County medical examiner Dr. Michael Sullivan had performed the autopsy and testified that she "likely" died in the early morning. Dr. Baden's testimony for the prosecution was that it was "much more likely" she died before 7:30 that morning. In arguing that the criminal case should be dismissed, defense attorney David Rudolf called the test (of the potassium levels in her retina) used by Dr. Baden "voodoo evidence."

The judge listened to the points made by both sides, then issued his ruling: the standard for medical testimony in North Carolina is "to a reasonable degree of medical certainty." Dr. Baden wasn't able to say he was reasonably certain, just that it was more likely. The judge ruled that wasn't enough to meet the burden of proof.

Without that key forensic testimony nailing down the time of death, the district attorney's office decided to drop the charges. That's always a tough decision, but the case was too weak to proceed without clear evidence connecting Friedland to the time of death. For a criminal prosecutor, once a case is lost and a defendant is acquitted, that case can't be reopened and brought again. Even if new evidence surfaces later, the case is over. A guilty defendant would be free no matter how convincing any new evidence might be.

So, Dr. Baden got on the plane home, and the district attorney dropped the charges against Friedland, deciding to wait until other evidence might present itself rather than risk an all-or-nothing gambit with less-than-solid evidence.

The specter of guilt, however, didn't evaporate for Friedland.

The police weren't ignoring another option: if Friedland wasn't there when she was killed, had he hired a hit man? That time-tested way to accomplish the same end comes with the added messiness and difficulty of hiring a hit man who won't bungle it, won't become a blackmailer and isn't an undercover cop. Nothing in the investigation put any flesh on the bones of speculation about a hit man.

The Civil Case

A criminal case demands a defendant. Without a defendant to carry the blame, the case is never over. Without a defendant, families and the community are left only with loss and unanswered questions. Since protesting his innocence hadn't moved the focus off him, Dr. Friedland knew the only way to reclaim his life was to show who had committed the murder. Friedland took the only route available.

In 1996, Friedland again hired criminal defense lawyer David Rudolf, who'd represented him on the murder charge. This time, they would bring a civil lawsuit—a very different creature from a criminal case.

In criminal court, the district attorney and police investigators call the plays. The standard of proof in a criminal case is tough: establishing guilt beyond a reasonable doubt. If the district attorney takes the case to court and loses, he gets no "do-over." The case is over. That's the double jeopardy from which the U.S. Constitution protects citizens.

In civil court, though, the standard is lower: jurors only need to be convinced by a preponderance of the evidence. In a criminal case, the state's evidence has to be weighty enough to tip the scales of justice dramatically against the defendant, because the outcome is weightier—someone could go to jail or even face the death penalty.

In a civil case, though, where only money damages are at stake (and not jail time), the evidence needs to tip the scales only slightly off balance. As a general rule, juries are more likely to take your money than send you to jail.

Marion Gales in prison for an unrelated offense. *Courtesy of* Charlotte Observer *and Charlotte Mecklenburg Library.*

The Friedland cases—civil and criminal—were attorney David Rudolf's first big Charlotte cases. A Raleigh-based lawyer, Rudolf would later become better known for defending NFL player Rae Carruth in 2000 for the murder of his pregnant girlfriend and, in Durham in 2003, defending Michael Peterson, the novelist accused of killing his wife at the bottom of the stairs in their mansion. That case has been explored in several TV crime documentaries, including a Netflix series, *The Staircase*.

Friedland and Rudolf filed suit against the man they believed killed Kim Thomas: Marion Gales, a local handyman.

Gales was on police radar from the first hours at the crime scene. A friend of Kim's had suggested officers should look at him. Gales's brother-in-law called police, too, the day after the murder, saying Gales wasn't acting right. Others pointed at Gales in later years, including inmates who said he'd admitted killing her.

When the civil suit was filed, the mood of most local armchair detectives was derisive ridicule. Going after some poor handyman who happened to work in the neighborhood and live nearby—a guy who couldn't afford a high-profile defense lawyer to protect him? How could he have pulled off such a vicious crime and left no physical evidence behind? Why would he commit such a crime? Nothing was stolen. She wasn't sexually assaulted.

Rudolf sought vindication for Dr. Friedland by presenting a public examination of facts that investigators had held close and offering another narrative for what happened in that house off Wendover Road. The downside was that if he successfully proved that Gales was responsible for Kim's death, a criminal prosecution against Gales was unlikely. Once someone has been charged, as Friedland was, a prosecutor knows later charges against another defendant will be met with skepticism and questions from defense lawyers, jurors and the public: You messed up before; how do we know you aren't messing up this time?

Proving to a civil jury that Gales was the murderer would, in some ways, set Friedland free. But it wouldn't put Kim's killer in prison.

The Evidence

With his signature preparation and attention to detail, lawyer David Rudolf built the case. Gales had volunteer lawyers who offered to represent him but were not well-matched against the trial-seasoned Rudolf. Those following the trial had to admit Rudolf was scoring points.

The *Charlotte Observer* published reporter Elizabeth Leland's four-part series about the case in 1995. In 2006, Cynthia Lewis, a chaired professor of English at Davidson College, dug into the case for a two-part *Charlotte Magazine* article. The title of the article—"Either/Or"—was apt, given the back and forth of the evidence developed over many years and in multiple investigations.

Imagine a line drawn down the middle of a legal pad. On one side is "He did it." On the other is "No, he did it." The facts on both sides piled up over the years:

* Gales lived a five-minute walk across Wendover Road from Thomas's house.
* A neighbor saw Gales in the area at 4:30 that morning; he looked "high."
* Witnesses said he owned handcuffs, though he said he no longer did. No one ever linked handcuffs to Friedland.
* That day, Gales was seen wearing bloody clothes and Docksiders, which would match the bloody shoeprint identified at the scene.
* The crime followed a pattern of Gales's past crimes, including breaking into houses where he'd worked and where, from outside, he could case the layout through windows.
* Gales had a long history of violence. In 1979, he broke into a house just down the street from Kim Thomas's house. When the woman surprised him, he shot her in the arm—a nonfatal wound but an incident that added to his already long prison record.
* Stabbing is a sign of anger (which could point to a husband), but stabbing is also a sign of frustration and agitation (which could point to a drug user desperate for cash).
* Nothing was reported stolen; Kim's purse, with her wallet, cash and credit cards, was hanging on the bedroom doorknob. But, following the murder, Gales had cash.
* Gales claimed he didn't know Kim Thomas, but a friend was at her house one day when he walked out of the woods from the direction of Wendover; Kim said he was a guy who did yard work in the neighborhood.

He cleaned her deck chairs and walkway that summer, and he could see much of the house's layout through the large windows.

* Police found no physical evidence (hair, fiber, blood) from Gales at the scene, and he was known to be sloppy at crime scenes, as evidenced by his numerous arrests. But the crime scene processing may have missed evidence, too, given some testimony from those at the scene.

OF COURSE, FRIEDLAND COULD have hired a hit man; he didn't have to be there on the scene. If he had, it's unlikely he would hire Gales (especially given Gales's penchant for getting caught) and even less likely he would risk suing Gales to tie him to the murder.

Cynthia Lewis, in her *Charlotte Magazine* article, summed up the difficulties of the civil case: "Sorting out the abrasive characteristics of Friedland's personality from any solid evidence of his guilt is as challenging as avoiding bias against Gales because of his history of violence."

THE INTERVIEW

In March 1997, before the civil case went to trial, another skirmish erupted in the headlines when Friedland agreed to an interview on Jerry Klein's WBT-AM radio show.

In a 1997 *Creative Loafing* article, Klein wrote that he'd been talking about the case on his show one night about a year earlier. The next evening, during a grocery-store run on the way home, a man approached Klein and introduced himself as "Ed," saying he'd heard the show. Klein said there was "something just a little bit odd in his demeanor. Something furtive, cautious." The man was tall, slender and dark, but Klein didn't recognize the man as Ed Friedland until later, as he drove home with his groceries.

"I thought about him all night. He didn't seem like a man who had slashed his wife's throat and left her laying in a pool of blood." Exactly what such a man looks like while shopping for groceries, Klein didn't say.

A year later, Friedland was scheduled to talk to Klein on his radio show about the pending civil trial, but the police department sought sanctions against Friedland and his lawyer for violating a protective order issued years earlier in the initial criminal case. A police spokesman said, "We can't talk about it; we don't feel anyone else should be talking about it either."

But talk he did. Friedland appeared on Klein's show on Monday, March 10, 1997. Klein admitted he hadn't expected to, but he believed Friedland. Everything he'd heard had cemented for him Friedland's guilt until they had a chance to talk—and in a very public forum.

In Klein's *Creative Loafing* article, after he'd culled through stacks of case documents, he said, "I continue to ask myself, over and over, whether I'm missing something, whether Ed Friedland has managed to con me—but I just don't see it. It would be easy to resort to some kind of journalistic shield of detachment, of impartiality, to qualify my remarks. But, after reviewing mounds and mounds of documentation—I can't do that. Put plainly, I started out believing Ed Friedland was a murderer who'd gotten away, but I don't anymore. I think he's innocent."

The Aftermath

Even though money wasn't the object of the civil suit, in October 1997, the jury awarded actual damages to Ed Friedland for the loss of his wife and punitive damages because of the egregious manner of her death, totaling $8.6 million.

That vindication was balanced by the hollowness of the verdict. As one juror acknowledged, they knew they weren't really taking away anyone's money—Gales didn't have any to take.

Gales had volunteer lawyers. In a criminal trial, the state pays for the defendant's lawyer if he is indigent and can't afford to hire one. Civil trials have no provision for court-appointed lawyers.

Gales's initial volunteer lawyers weren't as experienced as those hired by Friedland, so the verdict against Gales prompted yet more eye-rolling derision. No way the handyman who went door-to-door in the comfortable neighborhood could ever come up with a year's bus fare all at once, much less $8.6 million. But at least more of the story was now public.

Friedland moved to Florida, started a new practice, remarried, raised his adopted son, had other kids and lived his life. Few in Charlotte could know how Kim's death and the suspicion had affected his life or Kim's family.

Over a decade after the civil verdict, the case again hit headlines when, in July 2008, Marion Gales was arrested for the murder of pregnant, homeless twenty-seven-year-old Lacoya Monique Martin. His DNA linked him to her body.

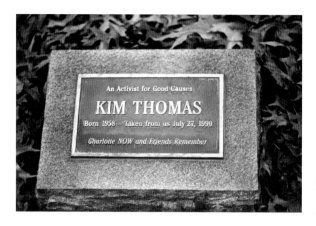

Friends of Kim Thomas planted a memorial tree in Freedom Park in 2013. *Photo by Libby Dickinson.*

Counting only from his most recent parole (which was in 2004), this was the ninth time he'd been arrested.

At first, he denied knowing the victim but then admitted to having sex with her. He denied killing her but then made an Alford plea, which allowed him to avoid admitting guilt while admitting the state had enough evidence to convict him. He was sentenced for voluntary manslaughter rather than face the risk of a stiffer verdict from a jury. In 2009, Gales's six-year sentence was extended under North Carolina's habitual felon statute, giving him a projected release date in 2025.

Kim Thomas's murder officially remained unsolved. In 2010, cold-case detectives announced they were following up on new evidence. In 2008, given the advances in DNA analysis capabilities, the handcuffs were scheduled to be tested for touch DNA. No results were released publicly, though, leaving another open question and another lesson in "what might have been" had the science been better at the time of the crime.

The house and the woods on Churchill Road were torn down to make way for denser infill housing.

In September 2013, Kim Thomas's friends planted a red sunset maple tree in Freedom Park to honor her twenty-three years after her murder. Her son, then twenty-four years old, came to town for the ceremony. He had been too young to remember her or the years when his father was charged with murder. One of Kim's friends noted that his "memories must come from people who knew Kim…and how much he was wanted and adored."

HERE AND AWAY,
SOLVED AND UNSOLVED

Like all towns and cities, Charlotte has its missing, those names and pictures that are printed on front pages or billboards or faded flyers, the stories we can't forget because they lack an ending, because we feel unsettled, as if part of ourselves is missing. Even if they aren't our children, they become the children of our hearts.

When a child safely goes to bed at night, or a twenty-something goes out with friends to see a comedy show and hit a bar or two or takes off on a summer educational experience in another city, parents simply expect them to be there the next morning or come home at the appointed time. No one expects a child to drop off the edge of the earth with no reason nor warning, no sign nor track—no return. Those stories frighten those with a child, a brother or sister, a young friend or loved one, because those stories tell us this could happen anytime, anywhere, to anyone. And we don't want to know that.

LOST HERE

Asha Degree

With her beaming grin, Asha Degree seemed like a kid we all knew. She disappeared from her home in Shelby, forty-five miles west of Charlotte, on Valentine's Day in 2000. She was nine years old. No one knows why, but she was seen walking down North Carolina Highway 18 about a mile from her house at 2:00 a.m. She may have been seen getting into a vintage dark-green early 1970s sedan similar to a Lincoln Mark IV or a Ford Thunderbird.

Three days after she apparently left her house voluntarily and was seen walking down the road in the middle of the night, her pencil and hair bow were found near an upholstery shop on Highway 18 near where she was seen walking.

Months later, her bookbag was found twenty-six miles farther along that same road, double-wrapped in plastic bags and buried in the dirt.

That's all we know. She was smart, did well in school and didn't seem the kind of kid to run away, and her family didn't seem the kind to harm her.

Over the years, her family has continued to plead for news of her, to keep investigators and the rest of us looking for any clue. Over time, she became a kid everyone knew. Through age-enhanced photos, we've watched her grow into a beautiful young woman, but one who is still missing.

The FBI became involved in the early stages of her disappearance and offered a $25,000 reward, which was added to the $45,000 in local funds. The Cleveland County Sheriff's Office continues to follow up on leads. Her parents have never moved and have never changed their home phone number, just in case she can come home or call. A Charlotte woman operates a blog, *Finding Asha: Shelby's Sweetheart*, to gather tips to help the police.

Asha remains a mystery we can't seem to solve. Detectives continue to meet regularly to review any new information.

Kyle Fleischmann

An accounting of how many young people populate the bars and restaurants in uptown Charlotte or the surrounding towns and cities on a Friday night would be hard to calculate, since they move from one venue to another. Those hundreds of folks come to enjoy a party, unwind from the workweek, listen to music and see friends. That one of them wouldn't make it home strikes an anxious chord, because after all, if it happened to one of them, couldn't it happen to anyone?

When twenty-four-year-old Kyle Fleischmann's friends left what was then Charlotte's Buckhead Saloon at Fifth and College Streets (now Fitzgerald's, a pub catty-corner from the back of the Blumenthal Performing Arts Center) at 1:00 a.m. on November 9, 2007, they expected to see Kyle again soon.

Kyle Fleischmann would have passed the statue of Queen Charlotte just before he disappeared. *Photo by Libby Dickinson.*

A sociable guy, Kyle wasn't yet ready to call it a night. But he didn't return home later that morning as expected.

Judging from his phone records, he tried to call his sister and father while at Fuel Pizza, just down College Street from Buckhead, while grabbing a couple of slices. He was probably trying to find a ride home but couldn't reach anyone. The early-morning temperature was below freezing, and video cameras show Kyle wasn't wearing a coat.

A cab driver saw someone fitting Kyle's description walking on North Davidson Street around 3:30 a.m., the same time Kyle's phone pinged off the cell tower in that area. That was the last registered contact with Kyle. He was just gone. His phone went silent. There was no sign of him.

In the following weeks, his family worked to keep his name and picture in the public eye. They hired a private investigator. Despite exhaustive ground searches in the area where he was last seen, no more evidence surfaced. The most likely outcome was that he was murdered by someone who took advantage of him being out alone on a lonely stretch of road after a night uptown.

Kyle's parents left Charlotte in 2010, eventually transferring to Florida with the same job that, in 2010, had brought them from New York to Charlotte, the place where they lost all traces of their eldest son.

LOST AWAY

Kristen Modafferi

Sometimes people leave Charlotte to visit elsewhere and disappear, so two cities feel the loss. At 3:00 p.m. on June 23, 1997, at the end of her shift, Kristen Modafferi left her barista job at the Spinelli's Crocker Galleria coffee shop in San Francisco's financial district. That was the last time anyone could definitively say where she was.

After her freshman year at North Carolina State, Kristen went to San Francisco to take a summer photography class at University of California, Berkeley. The day following her disappearance was to be her first day of class.

In a time before cell phones became ubiquitous, Kristen's father called her house to leave a message asking her to call home. When her parents learned her roommates hadn't seen her for three days, they quickly booked a flight from Charlotte to California to talk with the Oakland police and start searching.

The Modafferis made it to the Oakland police station late on a Friday afternoon, just as the officers were clocking out for their weekends. Her parents knew her well and knew she wouldn't just take off without letting them know. But Kristen was eighteen years old—an adult in the eyes of law enforcement. Of the roughly 600,000 persons reported missing each year, most of them safely return home. So, at first, the police weren't as alarmed as her parents were.

The National Missing and Unidentified Persons System (NamUs) maintains around fifteen thousand open missing-persons cases, because some people don't disappear because they want to.

The Modafferis' insistence that their daughter wouldn't stop communicating with them and she had to be at risk mobilized the police, but not without delay. When the officers got back to work on Monday morning, they began their investigation a few hours shy of a week since Kristen went missing and only three weeks after she had arrived in San Francisco.

Her coworkers weren't sure where she had planned to spend her afternoon or evening, but she'd asked for directions to Baker Beach, less than an hour's bus ride from the financial district. Did she go to a summer solstice party there, as rumored? This was unlikely, since the solstice date was June 21. Neither the party nor her attendance could be confirmed.

Bloodhounds tracked her from a Galleria bus stop near her job to the beach beyond the Sutro Baths ruins, a once-elaborate saltwater bathhouse built in the late 1880s and now a scenic oceanside vista on the coast. It, too, was a direct bus ride about seven miles across the city from the financial district.

Were the dogs wrong? Did she head in the opposite direction, across the bay, to the Oakland house where she was renting space for the summer? Her four roommates, all male, thought nothing of not seeing her. They all came and went on their own schedules.

Pictures of the dimpled brunette were plastered around the Bay Area, bringing all kinds of leads. A coworker saw her, about an hour after she left work, talking to an unknown woman at the Galleria. One man, John Onuma, put himself on the "persons of interest" list after he called in a tip about where they could find her body; investigation into his background turned up plenty of strange behavior, including claims that he'd placed classified ads and tried to coerce or rob women who responded and a report that he'd threatened to kill a woman and told her, "now you know what happened to Kristen Modafferi."

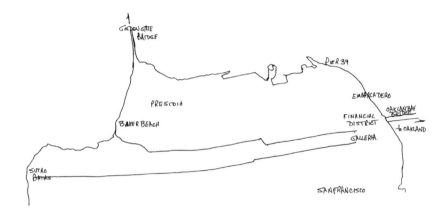

Map of the San Francisco Bay area. *Sketch by Cathy Pickens.*

For the Modafferis, an additional burden in the cross-country search for their daughter was the lack of support for missing adults. Kristen had turned eighteen only three months earlier and was not eligible for search aid from the National Center for Missing and Exploited Children. The Modafferis' Charlotte neighbor, Joan Scanlon-Petruski, started the Kristen Foundation as a national support group and resource for families of missing adults. Kristen's case was featured on *America's Most Wanted* and *Unsolved Mysteries*.

In 2015, investigators took a three-legged Labrador retriever trained as a cadaver dog to the Oakland house where Kristen had lived. According to his handler, the smell of chemicals left by human remains can be detected decades or even centuries later. This dog had successfully located remains of World War II soldiers.

When it barked repeatedly outside the rental house on Jayne Avenue, that signaled to Paul Dostie, the dog's handler, that they had something.

In February 2017, Dostie returned to the residence in Oakland with forensic anthropologist Dr. Arpad Vass, who studied at the University of Tennessee's world-renowned Anthropology Research Facility (better known as the Body Farm) with Dr. Bill Bass. Dr. Vass's research focused on isolating and identifying the unique sets of chemicals released at different stages of decomposition and identifying the presence of chemicals associated with odors of decomposition. Vass and Dostie identified human specific VOCs (volatile organic compounds), the unique chemical signature of human blood, in the area and linked it to DNA from Kristen's parents, but they found nothing else. Not every forensic clue leads to a resolution.

Over twenty years after their bright, beautiful daughter left her close-knit family to embark on an adventure, Kristen Modafferi's family and friends still pushed for answers to their questions from the other side of the continent.

Mary Shotwell Little

Sometimes, indefatigable investigators from other parts of the country come to the Charlotte area following leads, looking for answers to a huge headline elsewhere. In 2014, Ray Pate, a retired Atlanta police detective, asked his caregiver to drive him to Mount Holly in Gaston County to look for any news he could find about a Myers Park High School alum. The eighty-one-year-old Pate was dogging a case that had haunted him for fifty years.

In the mid-1960s, Mary Shotwell left Charlotte wanting to try life in a big city. Atlanta seemed safer than New York, her first choice, so she took a job at C&S Bank (which became part of Charlotte's Bank of America during its big merger phase in the 1980s and 1990s). She and Roy Little, a bank examiner studying to be an auditor, fell in love and married in 1965. Six weeks later, she disappeared.

The case has been one of Atlanta's enduring mysteries, one with strong ties to Charlotte. Mary Shotwell Little had dinner with a friend at the Piccadilly Cafeteria at Lenox Square after work. Lenox Square, in Atlanta's Buckhead neighborhood, was an upscale mall similar to Charlotte's SouthPark, though it opened in the late 1950s, at the time when Park Road Shopping Center was Charlotte's first shopping "mall."

In its early days, Lenox was an open-air space, like Park Road. Mary had shopped at the Colonial grocery store after work, getting supplies for the welcome-home dinner she planned for her husband the next night. He was due back from a business trip on Friday.

Mary didn't show up for work that Friday. Her brand-new pearl gray Mercury Comet wasn't parked in the Lenox Square lot near the grocery, where security had seen it the night before when checking the lot. However, when her bank supervisor arrived later that morning, it had reappeared, covered with a film of red dust, as if it had been driven on one of Georgia's red-clay dirt roads. It now sported a stolen license tag from Charlotte rather than her Georgia plate with the number 2829.

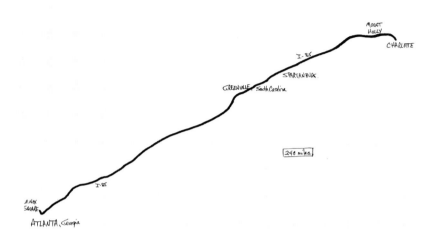

Map of route between Lenox Square area in Atlanta to Mount Holly and Charlotte. *Sketch by Cathy Pickens.*

Inside, some items of Mary's clothes were carefully folded between the bucket seats. A single fingerprint was found on the steering wheel, but police had no match. Blood was smeared on the steering wheel, the driver's-side door, inside the passenger window and on the front seats. What baffled the police—and roused suspicions about the scene—was how little blood there was. There was a lot of smearing but no more blood than would've come from a nosebleed. Was the scene staged? If so, why?

The mystery deepened when, on the Friday after her Thursday dinner at the cafeteria, her credit card was used twice at North Carolina Esso stations—once in Charlotte and once, twelve hours later, in Raleigh. The trip to Raleigh only took three hours, so what happened during those extra hours?

Descriptions given by gas station attendants in both Charlotte and Raleigh were alarmingly similar: a young woman, with some blood on her clothes, traveling with a scruffy-looking older man (or maybe two), who seemed to be telling her what to do. She hid her face. She didn't ask for help.

The Atlanta police worked every lead they could, first ruling out the husband, who had a solid alibi. They tracked the lead of a sexual-harassment complaint (related to another female) being investigated by the bank; they found no connection there. Mary apparently had a secret admirer over the weeks before she disappeared; her friends and coworkers told of whispered phone calls and flowers delivered at work, but Mary shared no details, and the florist connection led nowhere. Friends said she was worried about driving or staying alone while her husband was gone, but were those just ordinary nerves, or were they the presage of something more sinister?

The leads quickly evaporated—until May 1967, eighteen months after Mary Shotwell Little's disappearance, when Diane Shields, her coworker at C&S Bank, was murdered. Shields left work driving her blue-and-white Chevy Impala. In the early morning hours, her car was found abandoned near the drive-up window of a Sylvan Road laundry; her body was in the trunk. She had not been sexually assaulted or robbed of her diamond engagement ring.

Another woman told police she'd been approached by a man in the Lenox parking lot a short time before Shields would have been there, leading to speculation that her attack was a random crime of opportunity.

But, as with any case involving two attractive young women and whispers of sex scandal and odd secretiveness before their deaths, the stories grew. Some believed the two cases were related—after all, Diane had stepped into Mary Little's job after she disappeared. She was another small-town girl who'd come to the big city looking for a new life. She told friends back in Alabama that she was "working undercover" to help police with a case. Speculation was that maybe the detective working Mary Little's case had asked her to keep her eyes open. Had that gotten her in trouble? Or, as some officers contended, were the two cases simply not connected?

Who knows? People unrelated to the case became invested in it. Attorney Susan Carpenter Scott started her own private investigation, posting documents and inviting comments on her blog, maryshotwelllittle.blogspot. com. Ray Pate joined the Atlanta police force in 1960 and didn't work on either case. Still, he'd been on the force at the time, and in his retirement, when he was physically constrained as the result of a stroke, he spent his time investigating the case.

In 2010, Scott posted on her blog the transcript of a 1966 jailhouse interview done by the FBI, which led Pate to a house in Mount Holly. The inmate said he was involved in the kidnapping and described a small green house, a wraparound porch and a boulder in the yard. The house had long ago been torn down, but Pate wanted to see the area anyway. During his 2014 visit, he felt he'd found the right location, but it led no further than the FBI's 1966 interview had. His most recent post to Scott's blog, in April 2019, hinted at DNA leads and said, "Stay tuned."

Pate, Scott and others believe old cases can be solved. As plenty of other cases have proven, people get old and are more willing to share secrets—or perhaps too afraid to continue to carry them alone.

No matter where they roam, those who leave Charlotte and disappear still belong here. For every missing-person poster, there's a family tragedy, solved or unsolved. The measure of a place is how it cares for its children. We need to see the photos, tell the stories and share the weight of remembering.

SOLVED

Erica Parsons

In other cases, our hearts break because no one seems to care about the missing until somebody brave comes forward and says, "Hey, something's wrong." Viewers saw thirteen-year-old Erica Parsons on the evening news— tiny for her age, her broad smile crooked and sad—and feared what had happened. In the early reports, no one seemed quite sure when she'd last been seen.

The story unfolded over more than seven years and was circuitous, full of lies told with unblinking sincerity and stories hard to believe because they were too painful to be true.

Erica Parsons's adoptive parents, Sandy and Casey Parsons, had one story and kept repeating it: Erica wanted to go live with her biological grandmother, Nan, in Asheville. They hadn't even had to pack up anything for her, because Nan had bought her all-new clothes. They took her to meet Nan on November 19, 2011, and waved goodbye, sending Erica off to a new life with her real family.

The trouble with their story was that no one associated with the Parsons family heard from Erica for almost two years. No one could find anyone called Nan. Erica didn't take any of her favorite things with her when she left.

The Parsonses, though, continued to cash her supplement checks from the Department of Social Services for her special needs, not bothering to inform government officials they didn't know where she was and that she wasn't around to benefit from those monthly payments.

Their financial finagling with her checks finally landed the Parsonses in legal trouble, but only after Erica's older brother contacted the police, telling them she was missing.

That same brother testified against his parents, when they were charged with financial fraud, about the escalating physical abuse Erica had suffered for years within the family.

In the midst of growing publicity about Erica's absence and suspicions about their involvement, Sandy and Casey Parsons appeared on the *Dr. Phil* show in 2013 to exonerate themselves. Instead, they only raised more suspicions. During the show, Sandy agreed to take a polygraph exam administered by experienced polygraph examiner Jack Trimarco. His wife, Casey, declined, saying she was suffering pain from emergency colon surgery the week before; pain pills can skew polygraph results. Their answers to Dr. Phil's questions hadn't helped their case. On the next day's show, when the audience heard the polygraph results, neither Sandy nor Casey appeared. Casey's results showed him to be "strongly deceptive"—a clinical way of saying he failed.

As years passed, each article or news broadcast updating the case uncovered more painful details in the difficult life of the little girl.

Finally, in 2016, for reasons not reported, her adoptive father, Sandy, agreed to lead police to her body. He and his wife, Casey, were serving sentences for fraud for the $12,000 in benefit checks they'd cashed after Erica left their care.

Under police escort, he left the federal prison complex at Butner, North Carolina, where he was serving his eight-year sentence, and took officers to Erica's burial site near his mother's property in rural Pageland, South Carolina (forty-five miles southeast of Charlotte). Her autopsy revealed what little Erica had suffered in life and made readers wince. How could such abuse have continued for so long? How could a young girl be missing and not noticed?

The Parsons said they were home-schooling her, which wasn't supported by evidence, but that lie allowed them to keep her below the radar. No officials came to check on Erica. Why would they?

Once the autopsy results were available, the Rowan County Sheriff began putting together the criminal charges. On February 19, 2018, Sandy and Casey Parsons were charged with first-degree murder, felony child abuse and obstruction of justice. Prosecutors announced they plan to seek the death penalty; Sandy and Casey Parsons will be tried separately.

Dianne Gabriel

Monday, July 18, 1983, started what the Gabriels expected to be a busy week. Donald Gabriel left their Mooresville, North Carolina home (located thirty miles north of Charlotte) that afternoon to drive to Columbia, South Carolina, on a business trip. Dianne, his wife, had several real estate closings scheduled that week, as well as several scheduled showings with potential clients.

Dianne headed to her Davidson realty office that morning to work, then had lunch at the Pier Restaurant on Highway 150 in Mooresville. She met a couple at 5:15 p.m. to show them some houses, though she'd told them when they made the appointment that she had another showing at 7:30 that evening. She asked if they knew the man she was supposed to meet; they didn't. He apparently was a stranger to her, too.

Neither of her colleagues could go with her for her 7:30 appointment—a precaution the agents tried to take when meeting a new client. She stopped by her house, then drove away in her Buick Skylark with the Century 21 realty sign on the side.

Her husband came home two days later, on Wednesday, to find her missing. He found a note in the trash, which he passed on to police: "House Highway 150, Paradise Peninsula, Hogan Road, three-bedroom house, vaulted ceiling, partial basement." The note had a name and phone number and identified the house and a green truck.

An officer on patrol first spotted Dianne's car parked at the Pier Restaurant on the Monday evening she disappeared. The car was still there on Wednesday, July 20, with her briefcase and realty yard signs in the trunk. Her keys were missing; there were no fingerprints. The passenger window was shattered.

The following week, one of the many volunteers searching for Dianne found a plastic trash bag near a drainage ditch off Highway 150. The bag contained sexually explicit magazines, nylon rope, washcloths, a towel, plastic eating utensils, a ballpoint pen and—most ominously—a roll of duct tape and a piece of tape that had been circled and then cut through, as if used as an ankle restraint.

SBI latent print expert Ricky Navarro (who also found critical evidence in the Kim Medlin case) lifted prints from the bag and its contents and linked them to Johnny Joseph Head, who lived a twenty-five-minute walk from the Pier Restaurant and near the area where the trash bag was found.

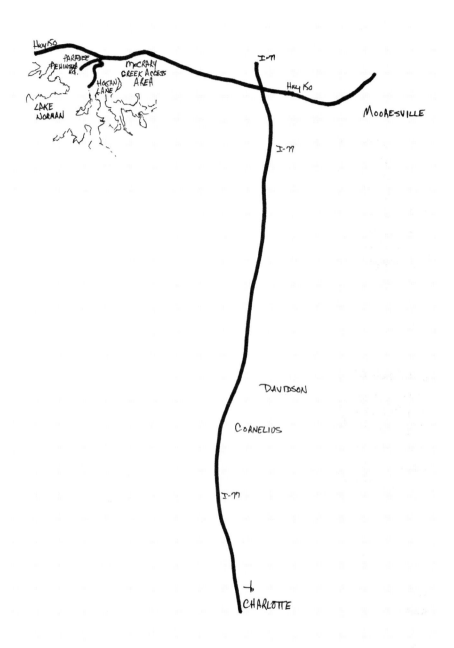

Map of Mooresville area where Dianne Gabriel disappeared. *Sketch by Cathy Pickens.*

In February 1984, seven months after Dianne's disappearance, a man walking in snowy woods found her clothing, shoes, handbag, keys and notepad near McCrary Creek Access Area and Paradise Peninsula Road, an area that had been searched when she first disappeared.

Extensive analysis by State Bureau of Investigation hair-and-fiber experts connected materials found at Head's house with material found in Dianne's possessions. Dianne's body was not located, but the prosecutor decided to proceed with the case based on the circumstances and on the hair and fiber evidence.

A year later, in March 1985, Head was convicted of second-degree murder. In North Carolina, second-degree murder is unlawful killing with malice but without premeditation and deliberation. This case was only the second North Carolina murder case successfully prosecuted without the victim's body; the first such case was heard in North Carolina in 1860.

An appeal would be expected in such a novel case. The defendant's attorney went back to seventeenth- and eighteenth-century British law for support, citing cases where alleged murder victims had returned from the dead:

> [D]efendant cites Lord Chief Justice Hale who in turn cites Lord Coke for a case in which a man was executed for the murder of his niece, who had disappeared. The niece had only run away and later returned to claim her property. Defendant also cites a case from 1661 in which a man was executed for killing a rent collector, who later turned up alive. In both these cases a strong reason for the "victims" disappearances was suggested by the facts: The niece had run away to escape beatings by her uncle; the rent collector had absconded with the collected rents.

The court said those cases didn't apply in this situation:

> There was no such apparent motive for Dianne Gabriel to disappear. To the contrary, there was much evidence tending to show strong motives on her part to continue enjoying the life she had been leading.

Head was released in 2001, sixteen years into his fifty-year sentence, still maintaining his innocence. Dianne Gabriel's body hasn't been found.

UNSOLVED

Some unsolved cases are particularly frustrating because of their senselessness and brutality and because they seem solvable but still have no answers.

Speros Kokenes

One of Charlotte's oldest unsolved mysteries is associated with one of its most iconic restaurants. In 1952, Speros Kokenes, son of one of Charlotte's first Greek restaurateurs, started his own Italian restaurant, the Open Kitchen, on East Morehead Street. Both longtime regulars and Charlotte newcomers came for heaping plates of pasta and the kitsch of political buttons and red-and-white-checked tablecloths.

Few patrons know that the restaurant introduced pizza to Charlotte. Speros's brother Steve brought the idea from Washington, D.C., when he returned home in 1954.

Some patrons know what happened to Speros one night in 1967. On February 12, after closing, Speros walked to his car, as always, carrying the day's receipts. Employees closing up for the night saw a man jump into the car with Speros and the car take off up Summit Avenue, the street running alongside the restaurant property.

An employee gave chase, then saw the car begin to swerve, a man jump out the back door and run off and the car hit a tree. Kokenes was rushed to the hospital with a bullet in the back of his head and the store's money and checks still in his pocket. He died soon after.

The police had a good lead on the killer. A woman said a man had tearfully confessed to her, but he wouldn't confess to the police, and the gun was not found. At the time, Captain Wade Stroud of the homicide unit said, "We're reasonably sure he did it." But the homicide has never officially been solved.

Bruce Ruffin

Sometimes, all the police have are theories. Whoever knows the story isn't telling it. Real estate agent Bruce Ruffin disappeared in April 1986. The police had learned about an argument and a likely shooting, and they began piecing together what could have happened even before Ruffin's body was found.

The first thing to appear was Ruffin's skull, found by a dog scavenging in the woods where Old Beatties Ford Road dead-ended near Lake Norman. Ruffin was last seen in a house on Bilmark Avenue, a street of small brick ranches in the Hidden Valley neighborhood.

Ruffin, age fifty, bought, refurbished and sold houses. He'd been in construction in Charlotte since the mid-1960s, when he graduated from North Carolina A&T University and moved from Greensboro to Charlotte. He'd had legal battles ranging from complaints involving his properties to a short jail sentence for making false statements about property he owned during his business bankruptcy.

He made a fresh start with his new business, Dart Enterprise, Inc., and had been successful enough to move his family to a house with a swimming pool in Cabarrus County.

From witnesses and physical evidence, police were able to piece together a timeline. Ruffin left his eight-year-old daughter about 7:30 p.m. on April 18, saying he'd be back soon; he had to meet someone. That meeting on Bilmark Avenue devolved into an argument, a struggle over a gun, and shots were fired. Police found broken window glass in the yard, apparently from a stray bullet.

Ruffin had been tied up and left in the bedroom closet. In the early morning hours, he was still alive. The bedroom had so much blood soaked into the carpet that police suspected his throat was cut. Blood on the kitchen floor suggested that the body lay there before it was moved to a vehicle and dumped in the woods.

Despite indications that colleagues knew who'd done it, no one talked and no one was arrested—the case remains on the Charlotte-Mecklenburg Police Department's "Cold Case Investigations" web page.

VICTIMS OF SERIAL KILLERS?

Charlotte is the birthplace of a mind-numbing number of multiple murderers—of the fictional variety. Novelist Patricia Cornwell got part of her crime education working the police beat at the *Charlotte Observer* after she finished Davidson College and before she moved to Richmond, Virginia, following her professor husband when he left Davidson to attend seminary.

In Richmond, Cornwell worked for the Office of the State Medical Examiner of Virginia as a computer analyst (carrying dead computers in the hearse, she once said). In Richmond, she found two principal inspirations—one was Dr. Marcella Fierro, a model for her books' lead character, medical examiner Kay Scarpetta; the other was a brutal series of rape-murders in Richmond.

In 1990, Cornwell's first novel, *Postmortem*, won five prestigious international awards for crime fiction, making her the first writer to sweep the awards in a single year. Cornwell's books remain on bestseller lists and launched the fictional phenomenon of forensic detectives, spawning television series such as the *CSI* franchise, which led to interest in nonfiction "science of detection" fare such as *Forensic Files* and *New Detectives*.

Coincidentally, Charlotte is also home to another big name in fictional forensic detectives. When publishers were looking for the next big forensic detective, Dr. Kathy Reichs perfectly fit the bill. She's a real-life forensic anthropologist who taught at the University of North Carolina at Charlotte and consulted with North Carolina's chief medical examiner, as well as the Laboratoire de Sciences Judiciaires et de Médecine Légale for the province of Québec in Canada. She was the 36th diplomate to be certified among the elite members of the American Board of Forensic Anthropology (which numbered only 119 in 2017). The *Bones* television series was based on Reichs's bestsellers.

That Charlotte would be a home base for two notable pioneers in educating the public about the intersection of science and crime-fighting was a coincidence that was especially ironic, since bestselling thrillers demand vicious, crafty killers—and Charlotte has, fortunately, seen scant few of those. One, Henry Wallace, is discussed in the chapter on crime-fighters. The other (or others?) left only shadowy evidence of their stays here.

The U.S. Department of Justice estimates that thirty-five serial killers actively operate in the United States on an average day, though estimates have ranged widely from thirty to one hundred active at any given time. How many of the nation's serial killers operate in this region? It's hard to say, though North Carolina never appears with California or Oregon on the lists of states where serial killers most frequently roam.

Serial killers tend to be stranger killers, and murders committed by strangers are significantly less likely to be solved than murders committed by family or friends. As the U.S. population has grown, the national clearance rate for murders has dropped from 93 percent in 1961 to 60 percent in 2016.

While most serial murderers have, statistically, been younger white males, that doesn't mean women or minorities are absent from their ranks. Early research by the FBI's Behavioral Science Unit (now the Behavioral Analysis Unit, or BAU) pointed to white male loners between twenty-five and thirty-five years of age and of average intelligence who tended to target people they didn't know from vulnerable populations (such as prostitutes, runaways, homosexuals and/or the very young and very old). The early serial killer profile omitted females and all ethnic serial killers, because those groups just weren't represented among the thirty-six serial predators interviewed in the late 1970s by Robert Ressler and John Douglas, the pioneers of the FBI's criminal profiling program.

The accepted definition of what a serial killer would most likely look like may have helped to mislead detectives when they were faced with Charlotte's most famous (known) serial killer—because he broke most of the rules. (See chapter ten.)

The scary truth, though, is that we don't always know who wanders among us. Charlotte has had one homegrown serial killer of note…but have there been others?

Sandee Cornett

On November 18, 1984, slender, brunette twenty-six-year-old Sandee Cornett returned to Charlotte after traveling to her parents' house for an early Thanksgiving celebration the day before. She and her fiancé had dinner together at her house in Charlotte before he left around 6:30 p.m. to drive back to his home in Greenville, South Carolina. He called her with their usual one-ring signal to say he'd gotten back safely.

Those were the days of landlines, when long-distance rates dropped after 11:00 p.m. Sandee would typically return his call after 11:00. When she didn't, he figured she'd fallen asleep.

The next day, when he still hadn't heard from her, he asked her neighbor with a spare key to check on her. Sandee wasn't home, but everything looked fine, with no sign of a break-in. The television was on. Her purse—with her house keys, checkbook and driver's license—was dumped out on the bed.

A closer inspection showed a few missing items: an answering machine, her ATM card and a dark-blue jogging suit, an outfit friends said she wore when she was staying in at home, not for jogging or running errands.

The insurance adjuster and part-time model always stayed in touch with her family and friends, so this was out of character. A formal investigation began. Sandee Cornett's ATM card was used twice after she disappeared. The police learned that a woman called Cornett's bank inquiring about the account balance, wanting to transfer money; the teller was suspicious and said they couldn't do that. In appeals to the public, police acknowledged that the woman seen at the ATM may not be involved in the disappearance and asked that she come forward, but the missing card and the unidentified woman yielded no leads.

Sandee's fiancé was closely questioned. The photograph of her heart-shaped face surrounded by a cloud of dark, shoulder-length hair was posted near restaurant cash registers and in businesses' windows all over town, but her disappearance remained a complete mystery. Her parents and neighbors kept her lawn mowed and things ready for her return even as months passed.

Seven months later, ninety miles south of Charlotte, seventeen-year-old Shari Faye Smith disappeared from her driveway in Lexington, South Carolina, while her parents sat in their house just yards away. When she didn't drive up to the house, her father walked out to investigate. Her car was stopped near the mailbox, but she was gone.

With manipulative cruelty, the kidnapper taunted her family with phone calls, talking to them about Shari. He had her write her last will and testament and mailed it to them. Shari was diabetic and needed medication and plenty of liquids; her family knew she was in danger.

Police from SLED (South Carolina Law Enforcement Division) and the FBI quickly mobilized, setting up a command station and phone tap at the Smiths' home. Even though they were able to identify the phone booths from which the kidnapper made the calls, he was always gone by the time they arrived, and the handsets were clean of fingerprints. He was enjoying the game.

Five days after the abduction, the kidnapper called and gave precise directions to where they could find her body. Until the end, everyone hoped she'd be found alive, but autopsy results indicated that she'd died soon after she was kidnapped.

On June 14, two weeks almost to the hour after Shari Smith was taken on a rural road, nine-year-old Debra May Helmick was snatched from her front yard in Richland County, stuffed into a car and disappeared. She was playing in the yard with her little brother. Her dad was in the house. They lived in a quiet neighborhood with little traffic. A neighbor saw a large man grab her. They tried to chase him. Still, she was gone.

The Columbia region was in a panic; girls of any age weren't safe, even on bright summer afternoons in their own yards.

Eight days later, Shari Smith's older sister got a phone call, telling her it would soon be time for her to join her sister and giving exact directions to where to find Debra May Helmick's body.

Ironically, long before days of searching cell phone records and cell tower pings, a handwritten phone number and landline address would be the killer's undoing. Embossed into the paper on which Shari was told to write her last will, SLED found the impression of a phone number. The number led to a home in Saluda, South Carolina, where a man had been housesitting for his boss.

When questioned, the boss recognized the voice on the recorded phone calls made to the Smith family as his housesitting employee.

On June 27, 1985, Larry Gene Bell was arrested in Columbia for kidnapping and murdering seventeen-year-old Sharon (Shari) Faye Smith and nine-year-old Debra May Helmick. As *Rock Hill Herald* reporter Andrew Dys pointed out, reports never referred to him by just one name. He always carried all three names: Larry Gene Bell.

Even though investigators questioned Bell using guidance from John Douglas, one of the FBI's top forensic profilers, Bell never admitted anything. The closest he came to a confession was saying, "All I know is that the Larry Gene Bell sitting here couldn't have done this, but the bad Larry Gene Bell could have."

Soon after his arrest, though, he began hinting that he knew something about Sandee Cornett's disappearance in Charlotte. Investigators discovered he had lived at an address nearby while working in Charlotte as an electrician. Sandee met him, once, through one of his Eastern Airlines work friends at a birthday party she hosted at her apartment for a friend.

Bell never gave investigators enough to link him, though it came out at his trial that he'd given rambling hints.

Sandee Cornett's body was never found.

Bell's connection raised other questions about other cases in Charlotte.

In 1975, a man approached a woman in a Cherry Road shopping center in Rock Hill, asking her to come party with him in Charlotte. She said no. He grabbed her and stuck a knife to her belly. Her screams attracted attention and summoned the police. He ran off. That man was Larry Gene Bell. In that case, ten years before his spree in Columbia, he pled guilty and was sentenced to five years for aggravated assault, immediately suspended to five years' probation.

In 1975, Bell was twenty-seven years old, lived in Rock Hill and worked at Eastern Airlines in Charlotte. Over the next few years, he moved back and forth between Charlotte and Columbia.

Rita Shuler, retired forensic photographer for SLED, wrote about Bell, citing the Rock Hill incident as his first confirmed assault. That one was crude and, fortunately, ineffective.

A year later, he attacked a University of South Carolina student and was sentenced to five years after agreeing to get professional help for attacking women; he served less than two years of that sentence. In 1979, he was convicted and given probation for making harassing phone calls in Charlotte.

Those are the documented crimes of Larry Gene Bell, cases in which he agreed to get counseling and his sentences allowed him second chances—as it turned out, he used them not for redemption but to hone his skills. Was he rehearsing and improving in still other cases? At least two other Charlotte women may have crossed his path.

Priscilla Blevins

Sometimes the missing come home, though not in the way—and never as quickly as—one might hope.

Priscilla Blevins, a Wake Forest graduate who had taught in South America and dreamed of being a United Nations translator, was last seen at her Tyvola Road apartment near South Boulevard early in July 1975.

Speculation associated Priscilla's case with Larry Gene Bell after he was captured in South Carolina, but officials never commented on any connection.

Statistics suggest that young people sometimes just pick up and disappear, which they have every right to do. Families find themselves investing their money and time pushing the investigation themselves. In Priscilla's case, her sister, Cathy Blevins Howe, took up the helm when her parents could no longer carry on researching the thirty-seven-year-old case.

In 2012, Priscilla's sister called the Charlotte-Mecklenburg Police Department (CMPD) cold-case squad just to see where the case stood. The detective she spoke to unearthed a 1978 article and talked to the private investigator the family had hired, and he did what detectives in earlier decades couldn't do—he sent a DNA sample from Priscilla's sister to the FBI's national database.

Active, current investigations take precedence over cold cases when allocating lab time, but three years later, the lab delivered a solution in the oldest missing-person case CMPD had ever solved. A familial DNA match was made to bones found in 1985 off Interstate 40 near the North Carolina–Tennessee border north of Asheville—150 miles northwest of Charlotte and ten years after Priscilla had disappeared. Dental records confirmed the identification.

Investigators were not able to determine a cause of death or piece together any more of the puzzle, but at least Priscilla Blevins's family had an important answer. People who are thought to be lost can come home.

Denise Porch

In the same month and in the same area where Priscilla Blevins disappeared, another young woman vanished.

Being a realtor or property manager is a high-risk profession. Most get training and establish procedures, because they recognize the risks of visiting empty properties with people they don't know. Few may know, though, the sad antecedents of those worries in Charlotte.

Denise Porch was the resident manager of the Yorktown Apartments on Tyvola Road when she disappeared on July 31, 1975. As with many Charlotte neighborhoods, the area near the intersection with South Boulevard has had its highs and lows over the years.

The facts have been rehashed in countless anniversary and "remember" articles over the years. Denise was a newlywed who'd just celebrated her first wedding anniversary with a beach trip. Denise had been seen mid-afternoon riding through the complex with a man, apparently showing him around. He drove a foreign car back when that was a distinctive description.

When Denise's husband got home from work, her Camaro was parked in front of their apartment where she usually left it. The note she routinely left to say she was showing an apartment was on the door. Her purse sat, undisturbed, on the table. The television and air conditioning were on, as if she hadn't expected to be gone long. The only thing missing was her master key and the register of open apartments.

Despite a nationwide alert about her disappearance and a lot of local publicity, she was never seen again.

Police investigated Larry Gene Bell, who had lived near the Yorktown Apartments at the time she disappeared, but they could never make a clear connection.

The police identified another suspect matching the supposed renter's description: a dark-haired man in his twenties or thirties, driving a foreign car, who had lived in the neighborhood until days after her disappearance. He'd been arrested in Greensboro and was eventually convicted of rape charges. But, again, no clear connection was made.

Was another killer operating in and around Charlotte at the same time, making women disappear? Or was Larry Gene Bell busier than anyone was able to prove? He was executed in South Carolina's electric chair in 1996, taking the answers he hinted he had with him.

ON THE RIVER

Murder trials are more satisfying when the bad guys are caught and properly punished, and all is balanced. When allegations of a wrongful conviction drape around a case, all is very unbalanced. Punishment requires certainty to be satisfying. Charlotte has had its share of stories with unsettled or uncertain endings, with none more compelling than what happened on the Catawba River one spring day in 2008.

Spring Outings

On May 5, 2008, two fishermen in Gaston County and a twenty-year-old student from the University of North Carolina at Charlotte started their days some thirty miles apart on opposite sides of Charlotte. By mid-afternoon, they would be inextricably linked. Key questions remain: Did their paths meet? Or were their separate paths simply confusingly and tragically close?

Irina Yarmolenko (Ira for short, pronounced "EE-ra") was known by her friends and family as smart, lively, energetic, generous and fun. She emigrated with her family from Ukraine when she was eight years old and was finishing up her college semester at UNC-Charlotte by running errands, getting ready to move to Chapel Hill. Surveillance cameras at businesses silently documented her movements that day—the ordinary wrapping-up stops anyone might make. Closed-circuit cameras clocked her visit to a credit

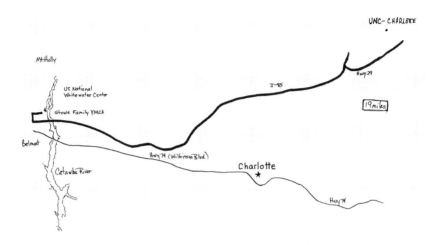

Map of the University of North Carolina at Charlotte and Catawba River areas. *Sketch by Cathy Pickens.*

union near the university at 10:18 a.m. Fifteen minutes later, she dropped bags of donations at the nearby Goodwill. She drove a couple of miles back toward the university to Jackson's Java (no longer in business at that location), where she'd worked as a barista, so she could say her goodbyes and leave a gift. She was transferring to UNC–Chapel Hill for her junior year.

From there, she likely hopped on Interstate 85 toward Belmont (twelve miles west of Charlotte), the only way to make the trip as quickly as she did. Those who knew her could only speculate about why she headed toward the river that day. She loved being outdoors, the spring day was in the pleasant seventies and she was an avid photographer. Her camera, which was left in her car, showed two pictures had been taken, but it had no film inside and no DNA on it, leaving more unanswered questions.

Whatever the reason for her trip, at 11:09 a.m., roughly twenty minutes after she left the coffee shop, a surveillance camera at the Stowe Family YMCA in Belmont recorded her car passing by. That was the last camera to capture her little blue car sliding out of frame. None of the cameras that showed her car that day could tell who was in the car—or even how many people were inside it.

Just past the YMCA, a dirt road turned right, toward the river.

Down that road, two Gaston County men spent the day doing what they spent lots of days doing: fishing along the Catawba River. The

111

Catawba shares the name of the Native American tribe that hunted and fished along its reaches between continually battling the Cherokee and Tuscarora tribes to the east and west. According to historian Mary Kratt, Catawba translated to "people of the river," related to a Choctaw word for "separated" or "divided."

The Catawba River starts in the Appalachian Mountains, supplying water to cities, picking up pollution and becoming a broader and faster separation as it flows south and east to form the wide, watery border between Mecklenburg and Gaston Counties. After it passes under the Wilkinson Boulevard bridge, then the Interstate 85 bridge, the Catawba disappears into Mountain Island Lake and Lake Wylie on its way into South Carolina.

Viewed from either the Wilkinson Boulevard bridge or the parallel bridge on Interstate 85, the river is bordered by thick green undergrowth and lush, well-watered trees, with occasional docks poking out from private homes. On the Charlotte side of the river sits the U.S. National Whitewater Center, with its man-made rafting rapids and mountain bike trails.

For locals, the riverbanks offer favorite fishing nooks that are hard for the uninitiated to find in the rutted tracks and undergrowth. The riverbank

The view from the banks of the Catawba River has changed little since 1915, when this postcard was produced. *Courtesy of Robinson-Spangler Carolina Room, Charlotte Mecklenburg Library.*

is wild and secluded there. But Mark Carver and his cousin Neal Cassada (pronounced "CASS-uh-duh") were old hands. They'd grown up together, raised four children each and lived close to each other. Both were disabled and could no longer work; jobs like theirs had been disappearing as the Gaston County textile mills closed one by one. Cassada had heart problems and couldn't walk but a few feet without struggling for breath; Carver had scars from carpal tunnel surgery and could no longer grasp heavy items. But they could stake out fishing poles.

Their fishing spot was downriver, past both the Wilkinson and the Interstate 85 bridges, just around a bend in the river on the Gaston County side. At the time, the Stowe Family YMCA was the closest "land" mark to the wilds along that part of the river. That May day, Mark Carver backed his SUV into their usual spot, and they fished from the open back of the truck.

At roughly 1:00 p.m., a man and woman on jet skis spotted something glinting in the undergrowth on the Gaston side of the river. It was a car stopped short of the water, its front end crunched into a tree stump. Later, the car's "black box" would inform an accident reconstructionist that someone had been sitting in the driver's seat when the car made its trip down the embankment.

No one was inside the car when the jet-skiers approached. The driver's-side door of the dark Saturn sedan stood open. They pulled closer to check things out.

A young woman lay on her back a few feet from the car, motionless. She had cords knotted around her neck. The weeds around the open car door were trampled flat. Her feet were pointed down the bank, tucked where weeds still stood thick.

The female jet-skier headed upriver to the boat landing to summon help. The man turned his jet ski in the other direction, flagged down construction workers at a new housing development and asked them to call 911. The 911 call was logged at 1:18 p.m.

Meanwhile, the two cousins continued fishing a football-field's length away from the car, separated by thick undergrowth, accompanied by the sound of construction in the new housing development and rushing traffic on the nearby highway bridge.

THE INVESTIGATION

The details of that day and the actions of Ira and the two cousins have been pondered by police investigators, prosecutors, defense attorneys, family and friends, newspaper reporters, amateur detectives and at least two television documentary crews (for ABC's *20/20* and NBC's *Dateline*). Those who have worked the case or followed its twists have their opinions about what happened. They have questioned everything—from whether Ira could drive between the university area and Belmont in twenty minutes to whether she could have tied the ligatures herself. Those who've debated the facts don't agree on how they fit together.

Ira Yarmolenko had not been robbed. When the local medical examiner, Dr. Chris Nguyen, performed the autopsy on the day after her death, he concluded that of the three ligatures, one alone would have caused her to pass out within seconds; she wouldn't have been able to tie all three. Two of the ligatures had clearly come from her car: a cord pulled from her hoodie and a blue ribbon torn from a tote bag and tied in a bow around her neck.

At one point that day, a local who knew Mark Carver by sight pulled up to the fishing hole in his boat to see how the crappie were biting. He said the guys were calm, not wet or muddy or agitated, like people who had just wrestled with an athletic young woman—just two guys fishing at their favorite spot. Though he saw them close in time to the death, the man was not called to testify.

The scene attracted a lot of attention that day, bringing cop cars and news helicopters. Police questioned whomever they could find near the scene, including the jet-skiing couple and Carver and Neal Cassada. The officers checked the two cousins' fishing licenses and asked if they'd seen or heard anything. Months later, as the investigation dragged on, Carver and Cassada agreed to come in for video interviews. Cassada took a polygraph and passed. Carver agreed but was never offered one. They submitted to cheek swabs for DNA and cooperated at every turn.

In his videotaped interrogation, even when an imposingly large investigator leaned into his face, insisting, "I found your DNA inside the car," Carver said, matter-of-factly, "No. You didn't find my DNA." Carver didn't flinch or falter.

Both consistently denied any involvement. They continued to assert that they had not seen or heard anything.

Investigators evaluated and eliminated eight suspects. Months passed with nothing new, no clear answers. Ira's brother Pavel Yarmolenko worked to keep media attention on the case, to shake loose leads, not wanting his sister's death to go cold and unresolved.

Then, in December, seven months after her death, the news broke: DNA results were back. Carver and Cassada were arrested.

In news footage, both men are visibly stunned.

The Arrests

Anyone who watches television crime shows or reads about crime, whether fictional or factual, knows that "DNA match" tends to settle the matter. It's done.

But even casual observers had questions and wanted details. Nothing about these guys—not their pasts, their personalities, their demeanor at the riverside that day or their actions afterward—suggested they could be killers.

As the use of DNA evidence first entered courts, the new science had to prove itself reliable. Though it was not the first DNA case, the O.J. Simpson trial was the one that brought DNA evidence to the public eye. Even though Simpson was acquitted in his criminal case, the extensive (and often mind-numbingly detailed) examinations and cross-examinations of experts popularized the new forensic tool for the public.

Most people understand the convincing and convicting power of a DNA match, even if the technical details of how a "match" is measured and calculated are hazy. Since 1986, DNA has pointed to perpetrators that investigators wouldn't even know to suspect, but, as it did in its very first investigative use in an English case, DNA has also eliminated the innocent as suspects. DNA evidence can also reach back and redress wrongs; since 1989, DNA has set free more than 350 wrongly convicted inmates.

Because of advancing lab techniques, smaller and smaller samples of blood or biologic material are needed for testing. The cutting edge at the time of Carver's and Cassada's arrests was "touch" DNA—only a few skin cells, such as might be transferred when an attacker touches the victim or something in her vicinity, was now enough to obtain a DNA profile.

In Ira's case, the new technology gave prosecutors a match. They arrested their suspects.

MORE QUESTIONS

Only the families and those closely following the case likely noticed when, two months after their arrests, the judge reduced the cousins' bond from $1 million to $100,000.

Why the generous bail reduction in a first-degree murder case? DNA testing of the bungee cord around Ira's neck revealed DNA from an unidentified person—DNA that matched neither Carver nor Cassada.

The men were allowed to leave jail and stayed on house arrest starting in February 2009, awaiting their trial date.

Neal Cassada never made it back to the courtroom. The Sunday morning before his murder trial was to begin, he collapsed and died just after eating breakfast at home. His family was convinced the stress of the pending trial was too much for his already weak heart. That left Mark Carver to face murder charges alone.

Five years after the trial, in a TV news interview, Judge Timothy Kincaid admitted that he'd thought the case against Carver was slim when the trial began. Neither Carver's nor Cassada's DNA was found on the cords around her neck. There was no DNA under her fingernails, and their fingerprints were not on her car.

But there were those magic words: DNA match, from both men, found in swabs taken from three locations on Ira's car.

Few court-watchers knew this bombshell match came from touch DNA, and even fewer knew its risks. While touch DNA technology represented a major advance in the ability to identify suspects, it also rang warning bells. Small amounts of skin cells or sweat can easily transfer from one person to another with a handshake or other contact, then be transferred by that second person to the victim or something nearby—such as a car. Samples containing a mix of DNA create particular challenges, and all three samples taken from Ira's car showed a mix from more than one contributor.

As the boundaries of science push further into the future, who determines when the science stands on firm ground—or when it has ventured into the weedy edges of what we know for sure?

Questioned Evidence No. 1

At Mark Carver's trial in March 2011, even the defense attorneys considered the prosecution's case weak. The state just didn't have much of a case, it seemed. Carver's defense attorney was so confident that he presented no direct evidence, instead relying on the weakness of the state's case, figuring the holes would be obvious to the jury.

However, given the evidence as it unfolded in the courtroom for family and friends, the jury and reporters, Carver's conviction was a shock but not a surprise.

After the trial, questions about the evidence quickly arose and became more insistent: Did the jury really get the full story?

The prosecution contended that the DNA got on the car when the cousins pushed it down the embankment, hoping to conceal the car in the river. But the three spots where DNA was found (on the rear driver side roof, the inside left passenger door handle, and the left passenger window) aren't good hand-holds for pushing a car.

At trial, no one presented a less sinister explanation for the DNA, but television documentaries and other reviews of the case revealed that investigators met with Carver and Cassada at their fishing spot that day; they held the two men's fishing licenses and shook their hands. Then, the investigators went back to the crime scene. Video shot at the scene shows some investigators not wearing gloves—and at least one appears to be touching the car.

In 2007, shortly before Carver's trial, Germany was dealing with the Phantom Serial Killer, an unknown woman whose DNA linked her to forty crime scenes, including at least six homicides, dating back to 1993. Police were baffled. How could a killer be so prolific across such wide geographic spans in so many different types of crimes?

Then, in 2007, tests results from a cold case added to the confusion. How could the Phantom's DNA be found on a male asylum-seeker's fingerprint card from 2002? When they were retesting using a different type of swab, the lab identified the culprit: the cotton swab. The Phantom's DNA belonged to a female worker in the Austrian cotton-swab manufacturing plant. The manufacturer defended itself: swabs were sterilized to kill bacteria; that process doesn't destroy DNA.

When such small amounts can be used to identify a suspect, cross-contamination is a dangerous pitfall. A 2012 California case may have been the first in the United States to demonstrate the risks of relying on small-sample DNA to put an accused person at the scene of a crime without other supporting evidence. Lukis Anderson, homeless and alcoholic, sat in a California jail for five months, accused of murdering a Silicon Valley millionaire, until a diligent public defender found that Anderson had been transported to the hospital the night of the murder. The paramedics who'd picked him up, unconscious, on a San Jose street, clipped an oxygen monitor to his finger in the ambulance, then clipped the same monitor on the finger of the murdered millionaire when they responded to that scene.

The chain of transfer from Anderson's finger to the dead man's was so clear that the district attorney dropped all charges against Anderson.

In Carver's trial, however, no one challenged the reliability of the touch DNA "match."

QUESTIONED EVIDENCE NO. 2

The second "uh-oh" in Mark Carver's trial came when the prosecution said Carver knew how tall Ira Yarmolenko was, even though Carver claimed he'd never seen her. Carver's interrogation video was not played for the jury, but the officer described the moment when Carver supposedly made that slip, describing how tall she was.

In his *20/20* interview, the judge said that once he'd seen both the DNA and the identification evidence, he felt Carver was in trouble, that "they gotcha." Later, the judge was shown the full interrogation tape by *20/20*; an investigator fed Carver the fact that Yarmolenko was small, was a "little thing." The investigator asked Carver, who was five feet and four inches tall, to stand and show him how tall she was. Even though Carver repeatedly said he didn't know, he followed the investigator's lead, stood and held his hands at eye level. Yarmolenko was five feet and three inches tall, an inch shorter than Carver.

At trial, the investigator's testimony didn't reveal the coaching given to Carver or the pressure to give an answer—or that Carver both prefaced and followed his answer with plenty of denials. In court, the investigator didn't repeat Carver's exact responses to the questions about her height: "Probably about right there…I guess, and I don't know…I just…I guess."

As the judge watched the video with the documentary crew, his expression registered genuine surprise. "It does make me question whether or not Mark

Carver did it," he said to *20/20*. "Certainly, I think that could've created reasonable doubt"—if the jury had seen it.

The jury never saw or heard about how Carver was led to understand Yarmolenko was small or how he answered that question. The jury just heard that he said he'd never seen her but knew she was small.

QUESTIONED EVIDENCE NO. 3

"Sound" evidence was the third evidentiary element about which the jury didn't hear the complete story. At trial, the prosecution said the cousins must have heard a struggle, that investigators stood in the two different places where Ira and the cousins were located and could hear each other when they spoke in normal voices. To those not familiar with the riverbank, it might seem reasonable that two men fishing nearby should have heard sounds of a struggle. Later tests suggest this is not the case.

The reports from posttrial investigations reported a distance up to one hundred yards between the cousins and Ira, but thick underbrush separated the fishing hole and the car. Even without the noise of heavy equipment operating at a nearby construction site, the traffic noise coming from the Interstate 85 highway bridge still blocked sounds in the later tests. Reporters couldn't hear each other until they yelled, and even then, they could not clearly hear each other. At trial, though, no one questioned the prosecution's witnesses about exactly where they stood or what they could hear.

UNRESOLVED

After a five-day trial at the Gaston County Courthouse and five hours of jury deliberation over two days, Mark Carver was convicted of first-degree murder on March 21, 2011.

Carver's story appeared on *Dateline: Mystery on the Catawba River* months later, in July 2011. His case was the first involving touch DNA to go before the North Carolina Court of Appeals, but the court denied his 2012 appeal, with one judge dissenting. In December 2016, ABC's *20/20* aired its episode about the case.

A woman who had no relation to anyone in the case and lived one thousand miles from Charlotte first learned of the case in 2011 on *Dateline*. In the years since, she has spent hours going through forensic research, online court filings and news accounts, fact-checking TV broadcasts and other reports, posting court documents and updating the FreeMarkCarver. com website, trying to help a man she is convinced was wrongly convicted.

In December 2016, attorney Chris Mumma, executive director for the North Carolina Center on Actual Innocence, petitioned for a new trial. Mumma and the Center accept only 2 percent of the defendants who seek her help and have had nineteen North Carolina convictions overturned. Following Mumma's court petition, newspapers ran headlines about pitched battles between Mumma and Gaston County district attorney Locke Bell over access to records and evidence.

In his now-famous videotaped interrogation, according to *20/20*, he denied his involvement in Ira's death more than fifty times. Before the trial, the prosecution offered Carver a deal: plead guilty in exchange for a sentence of eight to fourteen years, which could have meant even fewer years in prison. This was a sweet deal for a murder charge. Carver refused. He has been consistent and adamant: "I didn't kill her. I didn't touch her car." He's never wavered nor changed his story.

On June 5, 2019, thanks to Chris Mumma's work, Judge Chris Bragg held two weeks of evidentiary hearings and ruled that Mark Carver was entitled to a new trial. Carver was released on bond.

The prosecutor still believes the right man is in jail. But what if that's not true? If Mark Carver and Neal Cassada didn't kill the beautiful young college student, how did she die?

The not knowing is tragic. Even in an age with ever-expanding forensic science capabilities and cameras everywhere, a day beside the river can go tragically and mysteriously wrong for two regular guys who loved fishing and an adventurous young college student, all of them deeply loved by their families.

INTERNATIONAL INTRIGUE

Charlotte was built, from its earliest days, on transportation, commerce and courthouses.

Settlers built small wooden houses and cleared farms near the juncture of two major Native American trading paths that fell where Trade and Tryon Streets now cross at the center of uptown Charlotte. To give honor (and curry favor), the settlement was named for King George III's wife, Charlotte, of the German house of Mecklenburg-Strelitz.

The city's first charter, in 1768 (making Charlotte older than Raleigh and Atlanta), provided for a courthouse and a prison. Lacking an easily navigable river, the settlers knew legal matters and agricultural trade would drive the future of the small crossroads.

The first courthouse was wooden, with double stairs running up either side to a central, second-floor door. Underneath was a public market.

First came the trading paths from Charleston and Columbia, then the railroads and, later, the airport. The region's leaders have fought during Charlotte's entire 350-year history to secure the city's place as a transportation hub. Those early, wise leaders couldn't appreciate how the airport and courthouses would bring international attention to Charlotte 300 years later as part of its crime history.

These images show the exterior (*top*) and interior (*bottom*) of the replica of Mecklenburg County's first courthouse, which was located at the corner of Trade and Tryon Streets, that was created in 1976 for the U.S. Bicentennial. *Courtesy of Robinson-Spangler Carolina Room, Charlotte Mecklenburg Library.*

THE BHAGWAN

Cases of international intrigue may not routinely begin in Charlotte, but they have, in a couple of notable instances, ended here.

On October 28, 1985, an Associated Press photographer snapped an iconic picture of Bhagwan Shree Rajneesh (also known as "The Bhagwan"), the man with the waist-length beard, in the flowing gray-blue robe and knit beanie, as he waddled awkwardly with his wrists handcuffed in front of him, flanked by businesslike officers—one in a trench coat, one with a short shotgun. The prisoner gave a wan smile, his hand lifted in a slight wave.

What prompted an Indian philosopher's arrest on the tarmac in Charlotte unfolds like the plot of an ill-conceived thriller movie—if only it hadn't been real and ignited concern that this free-love guru with the beatific smile might be fomenting another Jonestown mass suicide.

The mass suicide threat turned out to only be an ill-spirited rumor, but the reality hidden behind rumor turned out to be the largest bioterrorism act to date on U.S. soil.

Rajneesh's road that ended in handcuffs outside two Lear jets at the Charlotte airport and a stay in Charlotte's jail started in India and moved to Oregon. On his journey, the guru attracted followers (called sannyasins), including many from wealthy families and at least one from Charlotte. Reports varied, claiming he had from 250,000 to 500,000 followers worldwide; a more accurate number is probably 10,000, with 2,000 settled in their self-constructed enclave of Rajneeshpuram in Oregon.

In 1981, four years before the Bhagwan (which translates as "adored one" or "god" in Hindi) landed in Charlotte, the populace in and around Wasco County, Oregon, had no premonitions of what was to come when Ma Anand Sheela, the Bhagwan's right-hand woman, bought the sixty-four-thousand-acre Big Muddy ranch for $6 million. She wanted to earn the Bhagwan's favor by creating a new settlement for him and his sannyasins.

The group left India, fleeing charges of tax fraud and public concern over the commune's free-love, sex-as-recreation, marriage-as-unnecessary-encumbrance belief and behavior. The ranch outside Antelope, Oregon, a city with a population of about forty, was to be their new center of spiritual enlightenment.

According to journalist Les Zaitz, "In India, the Bhagwan worked as a small-town philosophy professor until he found enlightenment paid better."

The Bhagwan then drew on Sheela's business skills and power-hungry drive to relocate his commune that espoused free sex, pop psychology and eastern mysticism—all dressed in shades of red and orange.

For many, the guru and his commune tapped into a 1960s idealism and vibe. The commune's wealth was stunning. Attracting rich members who were willing to contribute was a deliberate strategy. According to Win McCormack, Oregon writer, publisher, editor-in-chief of *Tin House* literary magazine and *Oregon Magazine*'s former columnist on the Rajneeshees, internal minutes from a Rajneeshee coordinators' meeting in 1982 noted: "Money [is] easier to get from those who have it."

A judge in Paris, hearing a 1979 case of drug smuggling involving a member of the group, said those in the group weren't "those who have 'end of the month' problems…those who break their backs to feed their families. No, these are rich people, not knowing what to do with their money, not knowing what to do with their lives."

Antelope, Oregon, is a ninety-minute drive south of The Dalles (pronounced "Dahls"), the Wasco County seat, a small city on the Columbia River about ninety minutes east of Portland on Interstate 84. Mount Hood is about ninety minutes southwest of The Dalles. The region is sparsely populated, producing mostly wheat and fruit.

The ranch sat on beautiful, rolling land. Sheela, in her zeal to successfully serve the Bhagwan by finding him a haven outside of India, failed to adequately investigate Oregon's restrictive regulations on population density for farmland. The commune's peace-and-love move to build a city for thousands quickly turned into an escalating battle between local and state elected officials and Sheela, the Bhagwan (with his ninety-three Rolls-Royces) and his dedicated followers.

In September 1984, four years after the Rajneeshees first arrived, a blizzard of phone calls hit the Wasco County Department of Health with reports of food poisoning in record numbers from restaurants in The Dalles. The Centers for Disease Control (CDC) found *salmonella typhimurium*—750 cases of it in a population of 10,000.

The Dalles had not seen a reported case of salmonella since 1978. Suddenly, the city was dealing with 750 cases linked to salad bars at eight different restaurants. How could that happen? The epidemiological study by state and federal officials found no common links in the water or food supply. The bacteria were found in different ingredients on the salad bars with no shared source or contact. The CDC tentatively identified the cause as contamination by restaurant workers.

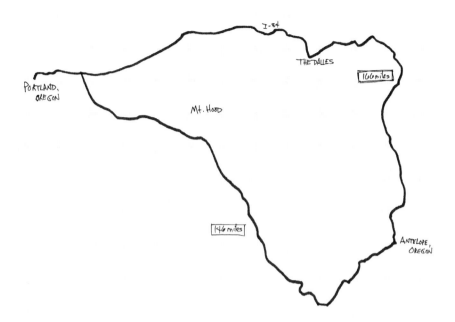

Map of the area near the Rajneeshees' compound in Oregon. *Sketch by Cathy Pickens.*

The true threat didn't come into focus for another year. During their four-year residency, the Rajneeshees battled with officials over land use (they began to build a city on land designated for "agricultural use") and immigration status (some sannyasins were suspected of sham marriages with U.S. citizens).

Their most controversial initiative was the Share-A-Home program, in which the Rajneeshees bused homeless people from major cities all over the United States onto their ranch and attempted to register them to vote. The Rajneeshees, who controlled the Antelope town commission, planned to take over Wasco County government in the next election to block opposition to their city, Rajneeshpuram.

The Oregon state attorney general filed a lawsuit charging Rajneeshpuram with violating the constitutional requirement of separation of church and state. The secretary of state halted the voter registration of the homeless. Both officials were criticized by the press, primarily in Portland, for not being tolerant and welcoming.

McCormack, in his detailed analysis of the case, said, "Media representatives—like much of the Oregon intellectual community in general—were in many cases actually sympathetic toward the Rajneesh enterprise, viewing it as both an exercise of the First Amendment right of free exercise of religion and as a noble attempt to fulfill certain mutually shared ideals of community from the 1960s."

Even as the Rajneeshees continued to "flaunt if not defy federal and state statutes," said McCormack, those perceived shared ideals meant "most segments of the press and authorities at all levels of government were slow to react." After all, the peace-and-love vibe of the 1960s was familiar and comfortable among intellectuals, especially in places like Portland.

It was not that no one in Wasco County spotted the malevolence behind the salad bar poisonings or failed to connect them with the Rajneeshees. In February 1985, five months after the poisonings, U.S. Congressman Jim Weaver spoke on the House floor about "the town that was poisoned." For months, he had been trying to explain to reporters and others how salmonella spread, that it couldn't show up in multiple restaurants in multiple foods that had no common point of contact or distribution. He tried to convince people that someone had to deliberately spread the bacteria to those eight salad bars. He told of a visit three Wasco County commissioners made to inspect Rajneeshpuram. Two commissioners who were not sympathetic to the Rajneeshees developed a violent intestinal illness later that day; one was hospitalized. The third commissioner, who was more accommodating, did not become ill. Congressman Weaver concluded his speech on the House floor by calling for an investigation.

Weaver was publicly and privately "taken to task" for his intolerance. He and those small-minded, insular people in Antelope and Wasco County needed to calm down.

Back in Wasco County, the longtime citizens turned out and voted in record numbers in the local election and kept control of their county government. Life didn't exactly settle down, but they felt a crisis had been averted.

A year after the poisoning, the truth came out—from a voice that had been observing a vow of silence. Bhagwan himself gave a press conference on September 16, 1985, a year after the salad-bar attacks and the Wasco County election. He openly denounced Sheela and her activities. In long speeches to his followers, with the press invited to attend, he heaped blame on her for the poisonings, her other destructive plans and for running Rajneeshpuram like a "fascist concentration camp."

Once cracks opened in the walls of secrecy, more of the inside story poured out. The attack, conducted in two waves, days apart, in September 1984, was only a test run; Sheela operated her own bioweapons lab, working on bacteria to poison the area water supply. The initial reasoning behind this was to keep voters away from the polls so the Rajneeshees could take over the county government.

Why was Bhagwan now calling public attention to Sheela's actions? Behind the scenes, the Rajneeshees were inside a tightening legal noose. The federal government had been investigating claims of immigration fraud, potential violence against public officials and irregularities in voter registration.

The government raided the Rajneesh Medical Corporation, the in-house lab where Ma Anand Puja, known as "Nurse Mengele," stocked pathogens even more deadly than salmonella. The salad-bar attacks were only a test.

Sheela hoped to weaponize the AIDS virus, a relatively new worldwide health concern at the time. The virus had not been isolated and identified until 1983. The Bhagwan had predicted that two-thirds of the world's population would die from AIDS. What better way to solidify his influence than to help fulfill that prediction?

Sheela was sentenced to ten years and served three before being deported. She moved to Switzerland and ran a residential care facility. The Bhagwan was deported, too; he died in India in 1990 at age fifty-eight. Rajneeshee believers are still active on social media, commenting on news postings about the group.

In 2018, Netflix aired a docuseries, *Wild Wild Country*, created by two brothers, Chapman and Maclain Way. The brothers were fascinated by the story that was little known outside of Oregon—and, as they discovered, largely unknown in Charlotte.

In a 2018 interview with Anna Douglas of the *Charlotte Observer*, the brothers' reactions to vintage 1985 news footage reflected both their California roots and their youth: they commented on a Charlotte man eating lunch with a cigarette in his hand and on Charlotte's man-on-the-street opinions, which ranged from a live-and-let-live, laissez-faire attitude to suspicions about the Bhagwan's "almost-royal lifestyle." Admittedly, the lavish lifestyle could be legitimately questioned; when the Bhagwan's two Lear jets landed in Charlotte on a leg of his failed escape, he was on one plane, and his "elaborate throne" was on the other.

Bhagwan stayed in the Mecklenburg County Jail while lawyers—including the Charlotte lawyer who'd once handled a divorce for a commune member from Charlotte—argued motions at the federal courthouse. News reports and stories from those eight days illustrate the city's enjoyment of a good tale. "We Bagged The Bhagwan" T-shirts enjoyed brisk sales. (Some are, as of this writing, being resold online.)

Hearings were held at the U.S. Federal Courthouse in Charlotte. *Courtesy of Robinson-Spangler Carolina Room, Charlotte Mecklenburg Library.*

The national news reported that Bhagwan had been offered a standard county jail breakfast: livermush and grits. When livermush—a uniquely Carolinian concoction—also appeared as a breakfast staple in Jan Karon's bestselling Mitford series set in a fictionalized version of Blowing Rock, North Carolina, the *Charlotte Observer* food editor took the opportunity to educate newcomers (and reluctant locals) on the best ways to fix livermush.

Bhagwan reportedly said no to both livermush and grits.

Sheriff C.W. Kidd Jr. also reported that Bhagwan said "no, thanks," to the thousands of dollars' worth of flowers sent from all over the country. Bhagwan had allergies. Reportedly, flowers were also sent to thank the sheriffs' deputies for their kind treatment of the commune's leader.

The national media called the atmosphere during his detention in Charlotte and his court hearings a circus. In Charlotte, folks tended to keep a sense of humor—maybe because they didn't know how serious it had been for Antelope and Wasco County. Or maybe they just know how to enjoy an odd situation.

The titillating tales from the sex cult eclipsed the story of the real threat that the group—or at least certain members of it—presented.

The sex headlines were much more interesting and easier to follow, even decades later. A democracy that welcomes other viewpoints and holds the freedom of religious expression as a foundational tenet has to also gauge the magnitude and severity of threats—and that wasn't easy in this case.

In a CDC report published in a nationally recognized medical journal over a decade after the poisonings, the authors asked an important question: "Can another outbreak like the one that occurred in The Dalles be prevented?" Their answer is unsettling: The pathogens used—as well as the more deadly ones found in the lab at Rajneeshpuram—were legally purchased from commercial biological supply houses. But, the report said, regulating the commercial sale of pathogens wouldn't have stopped the attack, because salmonella can easily be cultured from raw foods available in any grocery store. "Production of large quantities of bacteria is inexpensive and involves simple equipment and skills."

No one died in the salad-bar attacks. But salmonella isn't very lethal. The residents of The Dalles were lucky the experiment didn't move past the initial test run. The case raises sobering questions about how long it took officials and the public to put together the pieces, to see the threat for what it was. Would we see it more quickly and clearly now?

While Charlotte can remember the Bhagwan lifting his cuffed hands in a wave as he was being escorted off the airport tarmac in his exotic robes, the case also cautions that in the midst of welcoming, tolerant acceptance and an affection for entertaining headlines, vigilance is also required.

Viktor Gunnarsson

When the case began, it had no hint of international intrigue. It looked like a tragic small-town mystery: seventy-eight-year-old Catherine Miller was murdered in her Salisbury home, shot twice in the head with a .38. She was found on December 9, 1993.

At first, the connection to a Shelby man's disappearance was not clear. Viktor Gunnarsson, a forty-year-old Swedish native who had moved to the United States a few years earlier, was last seen on December 3. His last known location was at his girlfriend's house, where he had dinner with her, in Salisbury, a town forty miles north of Charlotte and home to the headquarters of both the Food Lion grocery chain and Cheerwine.

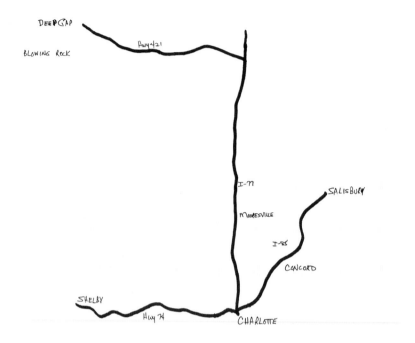

Map of Shelby, Salisbury and Deep Gap. *Sketch by Cathy Pickens.*

Investigators couldn't ignore the connection: Gunnarsson's dinner date had been Salisbury schoolteacher Kay Weden, daughter of Catherine Miller.

What did that connection mean? Was it just an odd and random coincidence that one woman would have a close family member murdered and a boyfriend disappear in less than a week?

Investigators didn't have to search hard to raise another question: Had Gunnarsson brought violence with him from Sweden? In his home country, Gunnarsson had been arrested twice for the February 1986 assassination of Olof Palme, the Swedish prime minister. Palme had been enjoying a movie date with his wife. He'd dismissed his guard detail for the evening. A single gunman took that unguarded opportunity and brazenly walked up to Palme on the street and and shot him.

Gunnarsson had openly criticized Palme for his pro-communist friendliness toward the Soviet Union and Cuba, so he was quickly arrested and held for a month.

Jan Bondeson's review of a book on the assassination, *Blood on the Snow: The Killing of Olof Palme*, explored a Sweden most outsiders might not know exists, a Sweden different from "the official version of the social democratic paradise: crime, drugs, alcoholism, police corruption and the kind of cronyism which arises when one political party—Palme's—has been in power for most of the last half-century."

Gunnarsson was eventually cleared of involvement, was paid a settlement by the Swedish government and immigrated to the United States in the late 1980s to escape the stigma of continuing suspicion. To date, Palme's murder has not officially been solved, and some rank it as one of the world's most important unsolved murders.

Gunnarsson's news photo shows a jovial man with a dark mustache and a broad smile. By all measures, he had settled into a quiet life in North Carolina—until his nude, decomposing body was found on January 7, 1994. A transportation department survey crew spotted his body in the snow near the Deep Gap ramp at the Blue Ridge Parkway over a month after he'd gone missing and a hundred miles up in the mountains from Salisbury. He'd been shot twice in the head with a .22-caliber weapon.

Was this political retribution? Were the Miller and Gunnarsson cases, after all, only coincidence? It took twenty-two months of twists and rabbit trails, but investigators methodically pieced together their case and made an arrest.

They later said that Lamont Claxton (known as L.C.) Underwood, a former Salisbury police officer who'd also worked law enforcement in North Wilkesboro, Lincolnton and Newton, had been a suspect from the first days of the investigation.

Underwood, who had worked as a resource officer at West Rowan High School before retiring in December 1993 on disability for a bad back, had

Scene from the Blue Ridge Parkway overlook. *Photo by Matt Benson on Unsplash.*

dated teacher Kay Weden. He wasn't taking their breakup well. He had confronted Weden's mother, Catherine Miller, on December 6, when she, her daughter and friends were having dinner at a local restaurant. He blamed Miller for the breakup. In front of Weden, he told Miller he wished something would happen to her so her daughter would know how he felt. By the time of that confrontation, Gunnarsson had been missing for three days, and Miller had three more days to live.

Investigators evaluated the Swedish connection, but they didn't ignore leads closer to home. Underwood was possessive and had reacted violently to Weden ending their relationship. She'd received anonymous threats. A drive-by shooting at her house left a .38-caliber slug embedded in the outside wall.

Gunnarsson's last meal with Weden had included potatoes; the cellular structure of potatoes can be microscopically identified during an autopsy, but potatoes digest quickly. Given the popularity of potatoes in Charlotte's regional diet, this offered no more than a possibility that his last meal had been the one he'd shared with Kay Weden, but it was a start.

Witnesses had seen Underwood driving slowly past Weden's house the night she had dinner with Gunnarsson.

Yet another lead pointed to her ex-boyfriend: Underwood had called the sheriff's office that night asking for a license check on the car parked outside her house. That tag was registered to Gunnarsson. Checking on an ex-girlfriend's new boyfriend isn't an appropriate use of DMV records, which raised more red flags.

Weden had received at least one threatening letter. Investigators located the typewriter ribbon used to create that letter and address the envelope to Kay Weden—it was on a typewriter at the high school where Deputy Underwood had recently worked.

The evidence drew a tight circle around forty-four-year-old Underwood. Investigators got a warrant to search his sparkling-clean 1979 Monte Carlo, where they found hairs on the trunk mat and, on the inside of the trunk lid, scratches and what looked like a footprint, as though someone inside had kicked the lid.

This became North Carolina's test case for the use of mitochondrial DNA (mtDNA). In the early days of DNA testing, mtDNA, which is passed only from the mother to a male or female child, was useful when only small amounts of DNA were available for testing. Despite his efforts to thoroughly clean his car, mtDNA isolated from hairs taken from the mat in Underwood's car trunk matched Gunnarsson.

The forensic evidence presented to the grand jury was enough to indict Underwood, and a jury convicted him of first-degree murder and kidnapping in 1997.

He exhausted his state appeals. A federal court agreed to hear his appeal and held that his trial counsel had been ineffective in promising to let the jury hear a witness that would exonerate him, then failing to produce that witness. In 2011, the federal Fourth Circuit Court of Appeals disagreed and upheld the verdict, saying that no matter what trial strategy was used, "the State's case against him was iron-clad and overwhelming." Underwood was sentenced to life in prison. While in custody, he died of natural causes in December 2018.

GREGORY CAPLINGER

Some cases start in Charlotte. The story of Dr. Gregory Caplinger started in Blowing Rock (ninety-five miles northwest of Charlotte), traveled through Florida to Santo Domingo, Dominican Republic, and ended in Charlotte in one of the courtrooms at the federal courthouse on West Trade Street.

Caplinger practiced medicine in Blowing Rock, a resort high in the Blue Ridge Mountains popular with Charlotte families looking for a cool spot during hot summers. He began attracting people from increasing distances as patients began to praise his healing gifts. However, his clinic didn't last long once the North Carolina Medical Board charged him, in 1989, with practicing without a license.

That news likely surprised his patients, because by the late 1980s, his curriculum vitae said he'd earned both a doctor of science degree (in biochemistry and immunology) and an M.D. in England, had worked in a hospital setting as a researcher and taught as a professor at a medical school. By his own questionable reports, he authored scientific articles, won international awards and was nominated for a Nobel Prize in Medicine for his groundbreaking work in immunotherapies.

Trouble was, the doctor wasn't a doctor. He didn't have a medical degree—unless you count his numerous mail-order degrees purchased for as little as $100 each from diploma mills in Great Britain—and he had not been licensed in the state of North Carolina. The impressive résumé was fabricated. "Doctor" Caplinger didn't just lack a license to practice medicine; he lacked any of the qualifications needed to even apply for a license.

Federal courthouse in Charlotte. *Photo by Libby Dickinson.*

Stephen Barrett, a physician who investigated medical scams, wrote on Quackwatch.org that Caplinger "made more claims and accumulated more questionable credentials than any other imposter I have ever investigated or heard of."

Charles Davant III, a Blowing Rock doctor who had helped put Caplinger out of business in the state, felt the consequences were too light. He pointed out that practicing without a license was only a misdemeanor in North Carolina, and "our state board couldn't revoke a license he didn't have."

After Caplinger's arrest, the man who had used injections and herbs to treat North Carolina patients for cancer and other serious illnesses paid his fine, moved to Florida and opened another clinic in the Dominican Republic.

No longer did the "doctor" limit himself to direct patient care, which can be time-consuming. Instead, he created an entire medical school, his own correspondence-course diploma mill, a pharmaceutical company and a magical elixir drug that would cure everything from cancer to AIDS to Alzheimer's.

Dr. Barrett, Caplinger's Blowing Rock nemesis, later crossed paths with Caplinger's new operation:

Once, I tried to visit his clinic. I was in Antigua on a vacation and, leaving the airport, I saw a sign that said "Home of the British West Indies Medical College."

"Take me there," I told my driver.

"That's it, Mon."

"No, I mean take me to that school."

"No that's it. Just the sign. There is no school."

Even in the days before the internet and sites like Quackwatch, Caplinger's clients and others were asking questions. Caplinger responded with voluminous lists of publications, including a textbook, covering studies of his ImmuStim immunotherapy and its effectiveness at fighting diseases. His brochures for patients included the latest buzzwords in cancer and AIDS treatments (such as interferon alpha and interleukin 2), over-the-counter treatments (amino acids, echinacea) and unfamiliar but medically-magical-sounding ingredients (cutis compositum, Engystol-N).

The people he preyed on desperately needed hope—and a cure. Patients found the theories behind his treatments convincing because they sounded so enticingly possible: stimulate the immune system with antioxidants and enzymes in unique, proprietary amounts to help the body itself fight off disease.

In 1999, the advertised cost of treatment at Caplinger's clinic ranged from $3,000 to $80,000. But, for the kind of results Caplinger promised his patients, many of whom were those given no hope with traditional treatments, this had to seem cheap. "Alternative treatments" offered solutions that U.S. doctors were too hidebound to try—or so his patients wanted to believe.

Patients who went to the Dominican Republic to be treated didn't find a state-of-the-art clinic in a shiny six-story building. Instead, they found a refurbished office building with an unsanitary, dingy series of rooms lacking hot water. Patients had to supply their own sheets.

Fortunately for Caplinger, some investors will part with thousands of dollars as easily as desperately ill people and their families do. When Caplinger began soliciting investors for his lucrative scheme, he found they, too, could be gullible—until the money got too big. When his money needs got bigger, suspicions grew.

He told investors the funds would keep his clinic running and buy new supplies of the drug ImmuStim, which he said he'd discovered himself and manufactured in the Dominican Republic. He told two Charlotte-area founders of the Diamond Group investment partnership, David Weekly (sometimes spelled "Weekley") and Harry Kampetis, that he needed $5 million to obtain a U.S. patent for ImmuStim to add protection to the Dominican Republic patent he claimed he already held.

Caplinger touted his British medical degrees, his teaching credentials and his professional honors. He presented financial statements from his clinic and predictions about the return on investment once the U.S. patent was obtained. As the years progressed, Caplinger's research published in nonexistent journals, fake degrees and imagined accolades proliferated.

In 1995, Weekly and Kampetis formed the corporation Immuno Pharmaceuticals, Inc. (IPI), with assets transferred from Caplinger's World Medical Services corporation.

They tried—but failed—to interest any large institutional investors, such as Shearson Lehman, in investing. According to a court opinion, with brochures and a video "describing Caplinger's clinic, the ImmuStim marketing project and ImmuStim's success rates on patients at Caplinger's clinic," they did entice fifteen individuals to invest $230,000 in IPI stock. Over time, Weekly and Kampetis also put in $1.8 million from funds their own clients had invested with their Diamond Group investment partnership.

Late in 1996, the two Charlotte investors learned of Caplinger's legal problems over his illegal practice of medicine in both Florida and North Carolina.

Within a few months, the two Diamond Group partners were facing their irate investors, whose money they had put into Caplinger's venture. In a two-year period, Weekly and Kampetis had sent almost $2 million to Caplinger and his clinic but seen no return on the investment; the two men hired lawyers of their own. The two men were charged with fraud, and in May 1997, they began working with the FBI with the promise of consideration in their own sentences.

At a federal trial in Charlotte in July 2000, the U.S. attorney carefully laid out a case against Caplinger, with Weekly and Kampetis as star witnesses. When the jury came back on July 25, after a seven-day trial, Caplinger had decided to not hang around to learn the verdict—he and his girlfriend had departed for the Dominican Republic.

A year later, he was returned to Charlotte; the judge gave him the maximum sentence for the mail fraud, wire fraud and money laundering charges, which was slightly reduced on appeal. The brazen medical fraud with an international reach died in prison in San Angelo, Texas, in July 2009 at age fifty-six.

CRIME-FIGHTERS

An exploration of historic crime cases should include an introduction to some of Charlotte's notable crime-fighters. Whether they were prosecutors or defense lawyers, police detectives or private investigators, forensic specialists or private citizens, Charlotte has an interesting cast of those who have helped to solve its puzzles, protect its citizens and redeem those on the wrong path.

A sampling of those who've served Charlotte can only be illustrative, not exhaustive, but the stories of two of them hint at Charlotte's crime-fighting colorfulness.

"America's Finest Detective"

None other than J. Edgar Hoover, as the director of the FBI, awarded Charlotte's chief of detectives Frank Littlejohn the title "America's finest detective" in a letter of commendation for his work in bringing to justice members of an infamous Chicago Prohibition-era gang.

Littlejohn is not well known in Charlotte today, but in 1933, as the police department's recently named head detective, he drew national attention when he led the capture of Chicago gangsters responsible for the daring robbery of a Federal Reserve money shipment.

THE GANG CAPONE DIDN'T TRUST

For the most part, Charlotte avoided the Prohibition gangsters who dominated crime news elsewhere in the country. New York, Chicago and even St. Paul (a surprising haven for gangsters, thanks to a mayor who said, "As long as you do your business elsewhere, you can stay here and we won't bother you") made headlines with the likes of Ma Barker, Machine Gun Kelly, Al Capone, Pretty Boy Floyd and John Dillinger. Charlotte, meanwhile, puttered along, minding its small-town business—until some of Roger "the Terrible" Touhy's friends came to town from Chicago to pick up some quick cash.

Touhy was a physically small man, standing about five feet and three inches tall, but he was a big man in the Prohibition Chicago beer racket. Known as one of Al Capone's biggest suppliers, he was also one of his biggest rivals as the two tussled over territory in gangland Chicago.

Touhy had been arrested for kidnapping brewery owner William Hamm in Chicago. The kidnapping was a "fit up," or frame, by Capone, who, tired of having to share the Chicago beer distribution market with Touhy, arranged the criminal charge as a little gift to his business rival.

Prohibition ended in December 1933, cutting into Capone's and Touhy's business interests in illegal liquor, but that didn't mean Touhy's legal troubles—or the antagonism of his gangster rivals—ended. On November 15, 1933, four men led by Touhy associate Basil "the Owl" Banghart waylaid the mail truck in downtown Charlotte on its way from the train depot. They grabbed Federal Reserve sacks that contained over $100,000 in cash (almost $2 million in today's dollars).

The big-city gangsters hadn't counted on the likes of Chief of Detectives Frank Littlejohn. Littlejohn was outspoken, unorthodox in his tactics and not always liked by his superiors, but he was effective at solving crimes. He knew the value of informants and had information months beforehand that something big was planned for Charlotte in late 1933.

After the gang struck, Littlejohn considered all the most likely escape routes from town and had officers scour those roads. Within a day, he located the getaway car, which had been stolen well before the robbery and abandoned down an embankment outside Charlotte.

From a torn laundry ticket stamped by a Chicago cleaner and found near the robbery scene, he tracked the gang back to Chicago. Two weeks after the robbery, as soon as Touhy walked from a Chicago courtroom after being acquitted of the St. Paul kidnapping setup, he was arrested thanks to Littlejohn's evidence.

Two of the gang members were convicted in an Asheville federal court for the Charlotte mail robbery and sentenced to thirty-six years.

Thanks to his friend Al Capone, Touhy stood trial for yet another "fit up" for the kidnapping of the brother of cosmetic magnate Max Factor, Jake "The Barber" Factor. In that case, Touhy was convicted and sentenced to ninety-nine years in prison. Decades later, the kidnapping was ruled a hoax. Touhy was released from prison in 1959 (after serving additional time for a prison escape); he and his bodyguard were both shot and killed a month later. Those murders were never solved.

As a result of his work on the Touhy case, Littlejohn, according to reporter John Kilgo, "made Charlotte off-limits to big time crooks and racketeers.… Littlejohn's fame spread rapidly and notorious crooks detoured around Charlotte rather than come in contact with him."

SMALL TOWN TO THE CITY

In 1917, Frank Littlejohn, a slender man with a big nose, came to Charlotte from Pacolet, South Carolina, a little mill village in Cherokee County, to work as a shoe-store manager. He joined the police force in 1927 for a temporary assignment, working undercover, then rose through the ranks to chief of detectives and served as chief of police for over a decade, from 1947 to 1958.

Until 1927, his only police experience had been watching stores for one dollar a night in tiny Pacolet. He later admitted to writer John Kilgo that he had trouble staying awake on his night shift, but his old bulldog would nudge him awake whenever it heard something.

Even as he moved into police administration, he never really stopped being a detective. His investigative instincts, his meticulous attention to fitting puzzles together and his extensive network of informants were his hallmarks.

Kilgo noted that the "man had more people volunteering him information than any policeman I've ever known.…[O]ne day when a murder was committed, Littlejohn received three calls telling who had done the killing before the body reached the funeral home."

Biographies accrete over time, calcifying into routinely told stories. Stories about Littlejohn were colorful and oft repeated, but details are tantalizingly scant about how he went from uptown shoe-store manager to federal undercover agent infiltrating the Ku Klux Klan in the 1920s to a temporary

Above: Standard Shoe Store, 32 East Trade Street, in 1926. Second from left is manager Frank Littlejohn, who later served as chief of police. *Courtesy of Robinson-Spangler Carolina Room, Charlotte Mecklenburg Library.*

Left: Frank Littlejohn (*second from right*) with detectives after J. Edgar Hoover commended them for solving the 1933 Touhy bank robbery. *Courtesy of Robinson-Spangler Carolina Room, Charlotte Mecklenburg Library.*

police officer in 1927, hired by the police to help break up an uptown prostitution ring. The part of the tale most often retold was his own career summary: "Hired for thirty days, stayed for thirty years."

Reading between the lines of news articles, Littlejohn didn't bow to power players or fret over hurt feelings, even when his career was at stake. About halfway through his time as chief of detectives, and about six years before he was named chief of police, he was fired.

The newspaper accounts of what led up to his firing were colorful and hinted at the politics playing out behind the headlines.

POLITICAL SHOWDOWNS

In August 1940, the county courthouse hosted the trial of what became known as the Dale-Wishart case, in which Fred "Jimmy" Dale; his wife, Rene Duffy; and Dr. W.E. Wishart, "late of the County of Mecklenburg," faced charges that they "willfully and feloniously, conspired, confederated and agreed together to knowingly, devisingly, and intending to cheat and defraud Rufus Bryant," a tobacco farmer from Clinton, in Sampson County.

Culling through the fancy court language, the essence of the case was that Bryant "carried a load of tobacco to the market at Durham," then set about procuring some womanly company for the night through the helpful offices of the hotel bellman. When Duffy, also known as Mrs. Jimmy Dale, came to his room, he assured her he wasn't the kind of man who normally did such things; he was married, and this was his first time.

They continued their assignations a few times over the next few months. Rufus, as she called him, learned she was poor and had some hard luck. He told her, according to his testimony, "I was not a rich man at all—I was a poor man and a hardworking man—that I could help her out some; that I didn't approve of such a life as that." He gave her a little money.

Early in 1938, she told him she was pregnant, and the baby was his.

Long story short, she wasn't pregnant. She and her husband had hatched a plan to get money from Rufus, "the old farmer." (Rufus was forty-two years old.) Dale even advised one of their friends, who was also "in the business," that she should go to North Carolina's Durham tobacco area and find herself an old farmer—an easy mark—like Rene had done.

Dale and Duffy successfully got $2,000 from Rufus before he wised up. Much was made about how she gained weight and easily looked pregnant, and there was a real baby, one they'd gotten from a girl who didn't want to keep it.

Dr. Wishart helped them procure the baby…but that's the real mystery in the case. Did Wishart know the Dales were using the baby to bilk an old farmer? Based on detailed testimony by another "working girl," the investigators and prosecutor believed the doctor was involved and indicted him.

The jury didn't agree. Wishart was acquitted at trial. Dale and Duffy were found guilty and sentenced to prison terms ranging from two to seven years.

As might be expected, Dr. Wishart bore Frank Littlejohn, the lead investigator, a measure of animosity—and he had enough clout to direct efforts against the chief of detectives.

MAYFAIR HOTEL . . . Charlotte, North Carolina

The Mayfair Hotel (now the Dunhill Hotel) was the scene of liaisons in the Dale-Wishart case. *Courtesy of Robinson-Spangler Carolina Room, Charlotte Mecklenburg Library.*

Littlejohn held his own animosities about the case, particularly over Police Chief E.J. Nolan's decision to reduce bond on Dale and Duffy after Littlejohn had put together the complicated case leading to their arrest.

The Dale-Wishart trial concluded in late August 1940. By early September, Chief Nolan had hauled Littlejohn before a civil service review commission, charging him with seven misfeasances. In a show of support, the civil review commission committed to pay for Littlejohn's legal counsel and expenses.

While international headlines reported on the London Blitz as "Nazis Smash Ruthlessly at Flaming London," local headlines covered the heated battle of Chief Nolan, certain members of the review board and the county prosecutor against Captain Littlejohn.

Chief Nolan expressly denied that he had suspended Littlejohn in retaliation for his dogged gathering of evidence against Dr. Wishart. But the hearing soon put the lie to that statement; one witness, Al Nelson, testified that he'd actually signed his affidavit accusing Littlejohn in Dr. Wishart's office.

The next day's headline left no doubt about the connection between the law-enforcement infighting during the fraud case and the charges brought against Littlejohn: "Dale-Wishart Case Is Linked with Littlejohn Hearing."

Littlejohn and his attorney refused to present evidence and were planning to mount a defense in court if the review commission found against him. The commission heard testimony and even had some good laughs at the implausibility of a couple of witnesses. Al Nelson, a character with a checkered criminal history, told convoluted stories about Littlejohn taking bribes; another witness claimed Littlejohn conspired in the running of houses of prostitution. Both of these witnesses, according to the *Observer*, "at times convulsed the entire council room, and even members of the committee laughed."

Chief Nolan testified about the bribes but admitted, when cross-examined by Littlejohn's lawyer, that he had relied on Al Nelson's statements and had never talked to Littlejohn or other officers involved in the raid during which Nelson claimed the bribes occurred. The chief admitted that he didn't know that Nelson's affidavit against Littlejohn was signed in Dr. Wishart's office in the Independence Building, and he didn't know Nelson previously had been convicted of perjury. When asked if that information would have made "any difference in his actions," Nolan said yes. The newspaper account left to readers' imaginations whether his answer was grudging or contrite.

The review commission promptly dropped three of the seven charges against Littlejohn. Of the remaining four, two more were dropped: that Littlejohn had refused to give an Officer Finlayson reward money he claimed he was owed and that Littlejohn had misled a grand jury about gambling on horse racing at the Sportland, a Charlotte club.

Littlejohn still had to answer to two charges in superior court: that he'd threatened Officer Finlayson and that he'd intimidated a witness in order to protect a female police officer (who was charged by a madam of extorting furniture from her).

Prosecutor H.L. Taylor, according to the *Observer*, "bitterly attacked Captain Littlejohn for not taking the stand" in the Dale-Wishart case and again "lambasted him for not appearing on the stand in [this] hearing and denying the charges. 'He sits supinely by and makes no denial from this witness stand of the charges,' Mr. Taylor said."

Littlejohn's attorneys pulled no punches, either: "Who is back of these charges?…We have Mr. Taylor, whose animosity to Captain Littlejohn is publicly known, acting as private prosecutor. We have Scarborough [the city attorney] who had at least two run-ins with Captain Littlejohn, acting as legal advisor to the commission. This same man testified as a material witness for the prosecution.…We have Mr. [H.L.] Strickland, one of the attorneys in the Dale-Wishart case, called as a witness for the prosecution, but withdrew because we were getting too close to the springboard of these charges, Dr. W.E. Wishart."

In a two-to-one vote, the committee found Littlejohn guilty of conduct unbecoming an officer, supporting his dismissal from the force.

The committee's spokesman, though, when pushed by Littlejohn's attorney, wouldn't say he was guilty of any of the charges. For the record, he would only say he was found guilty "in connection with two of the charges" but not guilty "of the charges."

Littlejohn didn't have to resort to defending himself in court. In November, the chair of the civil service commission dropped all charges against Littlejohn. Editorials in the *Observer* and other papers decried the attacks on Littlejohn and the desperate attempts "for several years to get control of the police department of the Queen City."

Headlines in January 1941 announced that Littlejohn was back at his desk. He hadn't been absent because of the review commission affray but because he had been helping with Roosevelt's third inauguration—one of six presidential inaugurations for which he'd been asked to help provide security thanks to his legendary ability to recognize well-known gangsters on sight.

Six years later, Littlejohn was named Charlotte's chief of police.

WELL-TOLD TALES

As chief of police, Littlejohn continued the pattern that had made his investigative career so successful: he stayed close to the criminal community and made use of a widespread assortment of informants. In 1957, one of those informants helped him arrest three men who were planning to bomb a black school.

The criticism of his tactics also continued: on the witness stand in a trial, the defense lawyer questioned him about the criminal record of one of his informants. According to writer Harry Wilmer, "Littlejohn exploded, 'Who do you want me to get to join an outfit like this, the minister of the Presbyterian Church?'"

Littlejohn once dressed in a suit and hat and went looking for a fugitive wanted for armed robbery. The man's friends were loyal and wouldn't rat him out—until Littlejohn expressed his dismay and pulled from his coat pocket what he said was an insurance policy. Too bad he couldn't find the man, Littlejohn said, because a relative had left him $10,000.

Littlejohn reportedly had the man in custody in a half hour.

He also knew how to use a flair for the dramatic when needed. Former *Observer* reporter Harry Hoover told how Littlejohn used a crystal ball and some voodoo spells he claimed to have learned from his nanny in South Carolina. When a woman was murdered in her home on Queens Road in Myers Park, Littlejohn figured it was a burglary gone wrong. One by one, he called the wives or girlfriends of his six most likely suspects into his darkened office and began his conjuring. One woman screamed, admitting her husband was the killer.

In 1958, Littlejohn's political opponents finally ousted him from office. He was battling with the city council over whether they could replace a police officer with a political appointee as clerk of the city recorder's court. In that battle, the politicians won. Just days shy of his retirement date, he handed in his resignation. When his recommendation for his successor wasn't accepted, he called the council members' actions a "dirty, rotten…retaliation stunt."

He didn't go without sharing a few parting salvos with the newspaper: "There will be an election in the spring, and if I know my Charlotte people, there will be some vacancies on the council in the spring." Three of the four council members were defeated in that election.

Littlejohn gave up politically charged jobs and opted to spend time with his much-loved wife, Elizabeth (known as Bessie), at their duplex on Greenway Avenue and plowing his farm in Pacolet. One news photograph shows him standing near a filing cabinet containing his cases, leaving us to wonder about the stories that didn't find their way into print to be recounted as part of Charlotte's colorful history.

Frank Littlejohn died in 1965 at age eighty. At the time of Littlejohn's death, John Kilgo, who frequently covered Littlejohn for the *Charlotte News*, wrote about once going to church with him at the House of Prayer on McDowell Street; Sweet Daddy Grace waved the lawman down to a front seat and told the African American congregation that "Chief Littlejohn is my friend and I want you to help him whenever you can."

Kilgo said, "I always accused the chief of having his police badge pinned to his heart." But Kilgo also knew him as "never giving an inch to a crook or a city councilman or a mayor. He enjoyed a good scrap."

DIFFERENT AND SIMILAR

In 1978, fifty years after Frank Littlejohn arrived from Pacolet, South Carolina, to run a shoe store, Garry McFadden got off the bus from another small South Carolina town to major in physical education at Johnson C. Smith University.

McFadden's hometown of Elliott, South Carolina, is located two hours from Charlotte, east of Columbia off of Interstate 20. While describing his arrival in Charlotte in the television documentary *Bad Henry*, McFadden said the second person he met after getting off at the Charlotte bus station was a woman in fancy dress who didn't look like she should be out on a rainy evening. "I gave her my umbrella." That's how young men were raised in Elliott, knowing "every woman in town was authorized to give you a whupping if you had it coming," he told *Observer* reporter Mark Washburn during an interview. McFadden didn't realize until later the kind of profession that would keep a woman out on the street wearing high heels on a rainy evening.

When he graduated from Johnson C. Smith in 1981, McFadden joined the Charlotte City Police Department.

McFadden, as it turned out, had more in common with former detective and police chief Frank Littlejohn than being from South Carolina. Both were known for understanding the importance of developing strong personal relationships within the community—relationships that aided in their investigative work.

McFadden and Littlejohn also both had memorable run-ins with their superiors: Littlejohn got suspended at least once and resigned days before his retirement.

McFadden told *Observer* reporter Mark Washburn about an incident early in his career. Working off-duty security at the Kroger on Albemarle Road, he drew his pistol on a car holding several people who had just run out of the store with a load of groceries. The woman in the passenger seat grabbed his arm as he reached in the window at the same moment the driver hit the accelerator. "I'm on the side of the car flapping like a chicken," McFadden said. He started shooting and continued to do so after the woman let go of his arm. The car "was full of bullet holes when it was found two days later."

No charges were filed against McFadden, but his deputy chief wasn't happy. After a period of tension and write-ups, the deputy chief confronted McFadden and surprised him: the deputy chief told him he was a leader, and he needed to act like one. As with much else in his career, McFadden took that lesson to heart.

The two detectives, their careers separated by decades, both got recognition from the FBI—Littlejohn's from J. Edgar Hoover in a letter, McFadden's as a commendation. But, as evidence of the depth of his belief in being a part of his community, on the weekend he was supposed to go to Washington, D.C., for the ceremony, McFadden had an engagement more important to him than an FBI commendation.

The story started in 1997. Andrew Ray, retired from the military, was an assistant manager at Hardee's on Randolph Road across from Cotswold Mall, working to pay his son's college tuition. Melvin Hardy, one of Ray's young employees, hatched a plan to rob the store and kill Ray so he couldn't testify about who did it. The killer and his accomplices were quickly caught, but that was little consolation to Ray's wife and four children. On an *Investigation Discovery* television episode, McFadden talked about how seven-year-old Angela Ray touched his heart when he visited her house. He stayed in touch with her and the family over the years, stepping in at times to help fill the void left by her father's death.

On July 30, 2011, instead of flying to Washington, D.C., McFadden donned one of his signature dandy "preacher" suits and walked Angela Ray down the aisle to give her away at her wedding.

The suit might mark one clear separation between the two detectives' careers. In Littlejohn's day, suits were the uniform for any professional. Newspaper reports don't talk about his sartorial choices, just about his big nose. McFadden, though, had a front-page article in the Lifestyle section of the *Observer* that discussed his "fashionista" status, the best places to shop for ties and how he learned the importance and power of showing up looking sharp. He also talked about shopping as a distraction and creative release from a tense job. Maybe Littlejohn, the former shoe-store manager, would have understood that, though no one ever bothered to interview him on the subject.

McFadden tells the story of meeting the first female Alcohol Law Enforcement agent sent to Charlotte, who spotted his blue eel-skin shoes and asked, "Who is this peacock?" He and Cathy married in 1989, and he still believes his pocket handkerchiefs, designer shoes and bow ties send an important message of respect and professionalism to those he meets.

DEADLIEST TIME

In the 1990s, Charlotte was growing. Between 1980—shortly after McFadden came to town—and 1994, the year Charlotte solved 100 percent of its ninety-six homicides, the population grew by 45 percent (to 470,000).

Growth typically brings new types of crime. No longer could Charlotte, even in its neighborhoods, pretend to be a small town like Elliott, South Carolina. Mamas couldn't keep an eye on all the young'uns. Everybody couldn't know everybody any more.

By 1993, the changes in the city were painfully obvious. Whether measured in actual numbers or per capita, 1993 was Charlotte's deadliest year, with 129 people murdered. *Observer* reporter Chuck McShane wrote a

Mecklenburg County's fifth courthouse and the old jail (now the district attorney's office) are pictured here along with the Bank of America Building and Charlotte skyline. *Photo by Libby Dickinson.*

twenty-year retrospective about that difficult year, when the crack epidemic was in full swing and young dealers and users were ruling the low-income housing complexes in Charlotte.

John Burnette and Andy Nobles were two police officers who had embraced the reemerging concept of "community policing." They walked their beat in Boulevard Homes, one of the most violent low-income projects in the city. They helped at cookouts and played basketball with the kids on the local courts.

Standing at the corner of West Boulevard and Billy Graham Parkway, Boulevard Homes was difficult to patrol—an area where police radios lost reception and hiding places were easy to find. It was the place where, on October 5, 1993, both Burnette and Nobles were killed in the woods, shot in the head with Burnette's gun.

Residents quickly helped identify the shooter; many believed the officers' engagement with the community spurred the residents to break what could otherwise be a protective wall of silence.

The neighborhood and larger Charlotte mourned the senselessness of the crimes.

In 2015, the Boulevard Homes area was rebuilt and renamed the Renaissance Community, with mixed-income housing, a spacious community meeting space, sidewalks, green space and links to neighboring educational and employment facilities. It also has streets named Nobles Avenue and Burnette Avenue.

In November 1993, a month after Burnette and Nobles were killed, another young man who had volunteered for three years as a reading tutor for children in Dalton Village, another troubled low-income housing area, was shot outside his girlfriend's apartment. Jeff Adams was a high school and amateur tennis champion, though few may know the connection between the Charlotte tennis center that bears his name and his random, robbery-related death. Adams and his girlfriend had just left a cystic fibrosis charity fundraiser when he was shot.

Charlotte was losing people who were trying to improve things, as well as people who had little to lose, all in the heat of a drug epidemic.

Though it took a while to recognize, 1993 was also the year police were connecting dots and recognizing that Charlotte had another big-city problem: a serial killer.

RANDOM EVENTS

McFadden couldn't know it in 1992, but a fellow South Carolinian had just moved to town to join his mother and sister, and the man would be at the center of watershed moments in McFadden's career and the criminal history of Charlotte.

In 1993, over 75 percent of Charlotte's record-setting number of murder victims were black. Among those victims was a growing list of young women.

People later complained about how long it took police to make the connections. Angry family members said the police didn't care because the dead women were African American—that if white women had been killed, the police would have paid more attention.

Admittedly, police were overwhelmed by the increase in homicides and lacked resources in both staffing and technology. But even with the benefit of hindsight, the links between the cases were hard to spot.

Even for the few investigators with homicide experience, the murder scenes left by this killer shared so few similarities that they didn't seem connected. Most were inside the victims' homes. One victim was submerged in a bathtub fully clothed. Several victims were clothed, creating the impression they hadn't been sexually assaulted. Sometimes, the killer brought the pillowcase or towel he used as a ligature with him; sometimes, he used what was at hand. Some scenes were neat and wiped clean. Others looked like a tussle had taken place. One body was dumped in the woods off Rozelle's Ferry Road. One stayed missing until the killer told police where she was. One he set on fire, disguising the scene so well that police didn't recognize the connection until the killer included her in his confession.

Because of the differences in the crime scenes, the story, as investigators saw it unfold, was a confusing piecemeal of clues. The case didn't present itself like a serial-killer movie or novel—there was no clear connection among the victims except their race; all of them were young African American women. There was no similar staging of the scenes to taunt police and tell them what they were dealing with, no trophies carried off, no letter written to a newspaper with tantalizing clues (a trope associated with the world's most famous serial killer, Jack the Ripper).

The police had none of that. They just had a growing list of victims—and a growing drumbeat of fear and anger in the community.

As 1993 continued, the killer got sloppy. The police couldn't know until after his capture, but his drug use was escalating. He no longer sought some inexplicable thrill; he needed money, and he got sloppy when he was high. He quit cleaning the scenes so carefully. He finally made some mistakes.

It was not until the murder of his ninth victim, Brandi Henderson, that detectives—all working an avalanche of homicides from Charlotte's deadliest year on record—began to suspect links in at least four or five of the cases... not nine of them, though, and certainly not ten.

It was not that investigators weren't trying to find any possible connection between the growing list of dead women and the scenes of their deaths, but the connections weren't surfacing.

The first hint of any connection was the strangulations. Strangulation is a relatively rare method of murder, a close-up, intimate method that requires several minutes of contact. Double ligatures were found around the necks of some victims. But none of the scenes showed signs of forced entry, so each victim had to have known the killer and let him in her house.

The police had consistently asked the victims' friends and family about any men the victims trusted enough to let into their homes. They found no crossover on the lists—not at first.

Brandi Henderson's boyfriend told them she would only let three men into her apartment. One was his friend, Henry Wallace. She was the ninth victim—and this was the first mention of Wallace's name.

Wallace was the only one of the three men named by Henderson's boyfriend who had any prior run-ins with the police; he had a shoplifting charge. When Detective James Stansberry pulled the booking photo, something struck him.

Stansberry had viewed an ATM video of a man using Vanessa Mack's bank card. Mack was the eighth victim. The picture was blurry, and the quality of it was too low for it to be usable for identifying the man's face—but it clearly showed the man's earring as he leaned close to the machine. He wore a Christian cross dangling from his earlobe that looked just like the one Henry Wallace was wearing in his booking photo.

The killer's second mistake was stealing a car from Betty Baucom, his tenth victim, to haul away electronic items he stole from her apartment. He ditched the car in a shopping

Henry Louis Wallace. *Courtesy of* Charlotte Observer *and* Charlotte Mecklenburg Library.

center directly across Albemarle Road from her apartment complex as soon as police announced they were looking for her gray Nissan Pulsar.

Was the killer taunting them? Or did he live so close that that was the easiest place to ditch the hot car?

As he'd done before, he carefully wiped away all evidence from inside the car. This time, though, he was sloppy. He missed cleaning off his palm print from where he'd closed the trunk.

Now, police had his name (from Brandi's boyfriend), his earring (in the ATM footage) and his palm print. Soon, they found out that the other women also knew Wallace, but in such casual or peripheral ways that he didn't come to mind when police asked the victim's loved ones about the victim's close friends.

Things moved quickly from this point.

Working backward, investigators found other connections between Wallace and the victims—through his job at Bojangles, his girlfriend, links to sisters or boyfriends. Wallace did his killing close to home: seven of his last nine murders happened within a three-mile radius of his home. Wallace worked as a cook and manager at several fast-food restaurants within a half mile of his apartment, and about half of his victims worked within a mile of Wallace's home.

RULE-BREAKING

The story was easier to understand in hindsight, after the killer was arrested and confessed, than it had been to unravel the unconnected clues.

In the "deadliest year" of 1993, the Charlotte-Mecklenburg Police Department (CMPD) started with only six experienced homicide detectives and antiquated technology and support systems that couldn't manage the flow of information from the investigation.

Also working in Henry Wallace's favor was the fact that he broke all the serial-killer rules.

Early on, before he became more drug-addled and frantic, he thought he was smarter than he was. For instance, he made the victims put their clothes back on so police wouldn't suspect rape; he didn't know police did rape kits as routine procedure (though DNA was still a relatively new tool, and testing took months).

Robert Ressler, a former FBI agent who helped develop the agency's criminal profiling program and is credited with first using the term "serial killer," appeared for the defense at Henry Wallace's trial. "If, in fact, [Wallace] elected to be a serial killer," said Ressler, "he was going about it in all the wrong ways."

Wallace fit the model in some ways: Most serial killings have a sexual motivation rather than a financial one (though he did steal for drug money), most serial killings are intraracial and most serial killers are moderately intelligent (rather than the evil geniuses presented in works of fiction).

Was he a rarity because he was African American? Academics continue to try to categorize and understand serial-killer behavior and motivation. The initial studies of serial killers conducted by the FBI's Robert Ressler, John Douglas and others focused on interviews with those who had been caught, and that group was white. Those men became the model for the serial-killer profile, although black, Hispanic and female serial killers do exist.

Are there differences in motives? Men and women who commit multiple murders differ in their motivations. For men, serial killing is often defined as having a sexual rather than a financial motivation, but women who kill multiple family members or those in their care often kill for embarrassingly small amounts of insurance money or inheritance, to hide small thefts of money or for obscure motives of power, a need to be in control or a need to rid themselves of a troubling duty.

So, serial killers—or "multiple murderers"—are not created equal.

Wallace needed drug money; he became careless, less likely to clean up the scenes. He killed two women in the same apartment complex on Albemarle Road within a day of each other, which helped narrow the investigation's focus.

Wallace's victims weren't stereotypical "serial-killer victims," either. They were not in vulnerable populations, such as drug users or prostitutes or living on the streets. Most were killed in their homes, indicating they knew or were comfortable with their killer. They were close to their families and friends. Most were employed or in school. In fact, Wallace met most of them at work or through women he worked with. He was just a friendly, helpful guy—a good listener.

Serial killers don't frequently confess, but Wallace did—in a ten-hour taped interview. As with many of the serial killers who do talk about their crimes, he remembered each scene and situation in detail.

The list of his victims came into shocking focus only after his confession. The *Charlotte Observer* collated the connections in a March 1994 article. Listed according to the dates the bodies were discovered (usually—but not always—the date of the crime), his victims were:

* Tashanda Bethea, eighteen, found in a Barnwell, South Carolina pond. Wallace had given her rides, paid attention to her. Wallace was twenty-four, almost at the opening threshold of a stereotypical serial killer's age range. (April 1, 1990)

* Sharon Lovette Nance, beaten to death and dumped in the woods. Detective Garry McFadden said she was the second person he met when he came to Charlotte, the woman to whom he'd offered his umbrella: "She was my friend." (May 27, 1992)

* Shawna D. Hawk, twenty, strangled in the bathtub at the home she shared with her mother and child. Wallace had been her manager at Taco Bell and a family friend; he attended her funeral. (February 19, 1993)

* Audrey Ann Spain, thirty-three, strangled in her Glen Hollow apartment. She worked at Taco Bell. (June 25, 1993)

* Valencia M. Jumper, twenty-one, strangled, her Greenbryre apartment set on fire. Her sister and Wallace's sisters were friends at Winthrop University. Because of the fire, she wasn't on the list of questioned cases until Wallace included her in his confession. (August 10, 1993)

* Michelle Stinson, twenty, strangled and stabbed in her Grier Heights home. She and Wallace were acquainted. Two small children were in the house, unharmed. (September 15, 1993)

* Vanessa Little Mack, twenty-five, strangled at home near Wilkinson Boulevard. Wallace was a friend of Mack's sister; Vanessa dated him once, and they stayed friends. Her baby was alone and unharmed on the living-room sofa when a neighbor came to babysit and found Vanessa's body. (February 20, 1994)

* Brandi J. Henderson, eighteen, strangled in The Lake apartments on Albemarle Road. Her infant son had a ligature around his neck but survived. Her boyfriend and Wallace worked together and were friends. (March 9, 1994)

* Betty Baucum, twenty-four, strangled at The Lake apartments. She was Wallace's girlfriend's manager at Bojangles. (March 10, 1994)

* Debra Ann Slaughter, thirty-five, strangled and stabbed in her Glen Hollow apartment. She lived near Wallace and had worked at Bojangles with Wallace's girlfriend. (March 12, 1994)

* Caroline Love, twenty, was not found until March 13, 1994, after Wallace confessed and led police to her body. She had worked at Bojangles. (Disappeared June 1992; found March 13, 1994)

Academics who have included Henry Wallace in studies of serial killings have often mischaracterized his past, saying his background was abusive or that he was not married or had trouble forming attachments. He was married, he had a child and he had a longtime girlfriend during some of the killings, although they had broken up as his drug use spiraled. Descriptions by those who considered him a friend or acquaintance don't jibe with those academic accounts, most of which were built on a psychological assessment developed for his trial defense.

However, some negative predictors existed. He did move from job to job; he was discharged from the navy for an off-base breaking-and-entering but was allowed an honorable discharge because of his eight-year unblemished service record. He sometimes described things in his life as going against him.

He also had the capacity to charm, to make women relax in his company. He was a good listener and helped out when they needed it. In early March 1994, he spent a Saturday night in the apartment of a female friend, drinking beer and watching television. She later told reporter Ken Garfield, "He was really respectful. Never made a pass, never cussed." Though Wallace didn't know it at the time, that was only a week before his arrest.

The following Friday, he called his mom in South Carolina just to see if she was all right and to tell her he was getting along okay in the big city. According to an interview with his mother, he said, "I might call you later." He had told his mom about his drug problems and got two dollars from a friend so he could go to the bus station uptown and buy a ticket back to South Carolina. He needed to go somewhere and get a new start. He seemed to know it was time.

"Y'all might not see me no more," he told friends on Saturday as they watched TV and shared a beer.

He was arrested that evening—March 13, 1994—at 5:00 p.m.

The case prompted changes in the CMPD and beyond. The number of homicide detectives increased from six to nine. Twenty years later, the detective unit had grown to include twenty officers. Both a cold-case squad and a missing-persons task force were added—an acknowledgment that solving old cases can help solve or prevent new ones and that a missing person may be a victim. The case also helped to emphasize the need for a DNA lab as part of CMPD's crime lab. Perhaps most importantly (and personified by how Garry McFadden had learned to support his victims' families), the department worked to have better communications with victims' families and with the community.

Doors to Mecklenburg County Jail, 2018. *Photo by Libby Dickinson.*

Charlotte skyline at sunset. *Photo by Daniel Weiss on Unsplash.*

Dee Sumpter, whose daughter Shawna Hawk had been left in the bathtub at the family's home, was an outspoken critic of the police department and of McFadden in particular. Shawna's murder was the first in what later became a clear pattern in Wallace's murders. Immediately after Shawna's murder, Sumpter held press conferences and called out the police for ignoring the deaths of young black women. At the urging of her friend (and Shawna's godmother) Judy Williams, Sumpter directed that energy and anger into a lasting project. They founded Mothers of Murdered Offspring (MOM-O) to help provide the advocacy and support they lacked when Shawna was killed.

Detective Garry McFadden credited this case with changing the way he worked—dealing with families on both sides of a crime became a hallmark of McFadden's police work. He retired from CMPD, and in 2016, the Investigation Discovery cable channel began airing episodes of *I Am Homicide*, featuring a few of the more than seven hundred cases McFadden worked during his career (with a 90 percent clearance rate). In 2018, *Bad Henry*, a documentary on the Henry Wallace case, aired on Investigation Discovery and featured commentary from McFadden, head homicide detective Rick Sanders and others.

After two seasons, no further episodes of *I Am Homicide* were scheduled because, in 2018, McFadden signed on for another job when he was elected sheriff of Mecklenburg County. He is now responsible for the region's largest jail population and a budget of over $100 million.

REFERENCES

CHAPTER 1

Albert, James A., J.D. *Jim Bakker: Miscarriage of Justice?* Chicago: Open Court, 1998.

"Attempt to Lynch Negroes." *Irish Times*, April 16, 1891. ProQuest Historical Newspapers, *Irish Times* (1859–2007), 6.

"Charlotte and Mecklenburg County Police History." *Charlotte Talks* with Mike Collins, WFAE. https://www.wfae.org/post/charlotte-and-mecklenburg-county-police-history.

Charlotte-Mecklenburg Police Department. "Our Organization." Accessed October 25, 2018. https://charlottenc.gov/CMPD/Organization/Pages/default.aspx.

"Fatal Detection: Solving Killings in NC." *Charlotte Observer*, April 18, 1988, 4A.

Funk, Tim. "Jim Bakker's Theme Park Was Like a Christian Disneyland. Here's What Happened to It." *Charlotte Observer*, March 17, 2018 (updated March 20, 2018). https://www.charlotteobserver.com/living/religion/article205362719.html.

"Gross Lapse: A Murder Record Is Dished up without Charlotte." *Charlotte News*, December 2, 1940.

Hanchett, Tom. *Sorting Out the New South City: Race, Class, and Urban Development in Charlotte, 1875–1975.* Chapel Hill: University of North Carolina Press, 1998.

Henderson, Bruce. "A Showman to the End, His Gorilla Suits Launched a Costume Empire." *Charlotte Observer*, September 25, 2017. https://www.charlotteobserver.com/news/local/article175326976.html.

Jameson, Tonya. "Stomping on a Legend: Bigfoot, or a Costume?" *Charlotte Observer*, May 11, 2004, 1D.

Janes, Théoden. "Will Loomis Fargo Heist Movie 'Masterminds' Be Worth (Loooong) Wait?" *Charlotte Observer*, August 14, 2016, 3C.

"Little Chicago: Murders, Rape and Robberies Shame the City of Churches." *Charlotte News*, February 11, 1961, 3A.

Moore, David Aaron. *Charlotte: Murder, Mystery and Mayhem*. Charleston, SC: The History Press, 2008.

———. "Question the Queen City: The Story of Nellie Freeman, a.k.a. 'Razor Girl.'" *Creative Loafing Charlotte*, September 27, 2013. http://clclt.com/thelog/archives/2013/09/27/question-the-queen-city-the-story-of-nellie-freeman-aka-razor-girl.

Morganthall, Judy. "Night Owl: Philip Morris Runs His Charlotte-Based Costume-Business Empire in the Wee Hours." *SouthPark Magazine*, 2006.

"Murder of John B. Mocca." *Charlotte Democrat*, April 14, 1891.

Pickens, Cathy. "Charlotte Noir." In *27 Views of Charlotte*, 78–89. Hillsborough, NC: Eno Press, 2014.

Price, Mark. "Charlotte Is on the List of 'Deadliest U.S. Cities.'" *Charlotte Observer*, February 12, 2018. https://www.charlotteobserver.com/news/local/article199620439.html.

Semuels, Alana. "Segregation Had to Be Invented." *The Atlantic*, February 17, 2017. https://www.theatlantic.com/business/archive/2017/02/segregation-invented/517158/.

Shepard, Charles E. *Forgiven: The Rise and Fall of Jim Bakker and the PTL Ministry*. New York: Atlantic Monthly Press, 1989.

Sumner, Ryan L. *Charlotte and Mecklenburg County Police*. Charleston, SC: Arcadia Publishing, 2010.

Tidwell, Gary. *Anatomy of a Fraud: Inside the Finances of the PTL Ministries*. New York: John Wiley & Sons, 1993.

Williams, Stephanie Burt. *Wicked Charlotte: The Sordid Side of the Queen City*. Charleston, SC: The History Press, 2006.

CHAPTER 2

Southern Charmer and Spy: Gaston Means

Bryk, William. "Conman of the Century." *New York Press*, July 8, 2003. http://nypress.com/conman-of-the-century.

Felder v. United States. 9 F.2d 872 (2nd Cir. 1925).

Franklin, Charles. "Teapot Dome." In *They Walked a Crooked Mile*, 219–241. New York: Hart, 1969.

Hoyt, Edwin P. *Spectacular Rogue: Gaston B. Means*. Indianapolis, IN, and New York: Bobbs-Merrill, 1963.

Means, Gaston B., as told to May Dixon Thacker. *The Strange Death of President Harding*. New York: Guild Publishing, 1930.

Moger, Art. "The Incredible Gaston B. Means, 'the Greatest Faker of Them All." In *Pros and Cons*, 219–241. Greenwich, CT: Fawcett, 1975.

Sifakis, Carl. *Frauds, Deceptions and Swindles*. New York: Checkmark Books, 2001.

Whitaker v. United States, 72 F.2d 739 (D.C. Cir. 1934).

When Greed Turns Deadly: Joey Caldwell

Cox, Clark. *Deadly Greed*. Boone, NC: High Country Publishers, 2003.

FROM THE *CHARLOTTE OBSERVER* (IN CHRONOLOGICAL ORDER):

Williams, Paige. "Town Asks: Who Would Kill Mother, Son?" April 14, 1991, 3B.

———. "The Talk of the County: Hamlet Slayings Remain a Mystery." April 15, 1991, 1A.

Menn, Joseph, and Paige Williams. "Victim Was Set to Testify: $2 Million Suit Alleges Conspiracy." April 16, 1991, 1A.

Menn, Joseph. "Police Rule Out Robbery Motive in Hamlet Killings but Little Else." April 18, 1991, 2B.

———. "Man Killed Was Insured for $2 Million: $2 Million Policy Getting a Hard Look." July 13, 1991, 1A.

———. "Life Insurance Claim, Lawsuits over Sports-Drink Firm Settled." September 20, 1991, 1D.

Wilson, Sue Price. "Unsolved Murders Haunt SBI Team: About Half of Cases Assigned to Special Unit Elude Answers." January 4, 1993, 4C.

———. "Trial Opens Next Week in Unusual Fraud Case." August 21, 1993, 1D.

———. "Caldwell's Wife Tells Court How They Plotted to Kill McEachern." August 25, 1993, 1D.

———. "Accused Businessman Expected to Testify." August 27, 1993, 1D.

———. "Joey Caldwell Denies Role in Killing Mortician, Mom." August 28, 1993, 1D.

O'Brien, Kevin. "Trial Witness Placed on Leave as Teacher." September 1, 1993, 1C.

———. "Caldwell Convicted of 57 Counts." September 2, 1993, 1C.

———. "Caldwell Is Apparent Jail Suicide." September 3, 1993, 1C.

———. "Dreams of Riches, Acts of Betrayal." November 28, 1993, 1A.

———. "Alibis Stop Investigators Like a Concrete Block." November 29, 1993, 1A.

———. "Client X Gives Investigators Break Needed to Solve Case." November 30, 1993, 1A.

———. "Woman Whose Testimony Helped Convict Her Husband in Murders Enters Guilty Pleas." January 6, 1994, 3C.

Hechinger, John. "Barbara Caldwell Gets 5 Years." April 1, 1994, 1C.

CHAPTER 3

"After Decades of Lies 'and Taste of Freedom' Doctor Returns to Prison." *Pocono Record*, August 22, 2002 (updated January 7, 2011). http://www.poconorecord.com/article/20020825/News/308259998.

Commonwealth v. Scher, Superior Court of Pennsylvania, June 7, 1999. https://caselaw.findlaw.com/pa-superior-court/1396400.html. [Held that delay in bringing case was improper.]

Commonwealth v. Scher, Supreme Court of Pennsylvania, August 20, 2002. https://caselaw.findlaw.com/pa-supreme-court/1464236.html. [Overturned Superior Court; delay not improper.]

Eftimiades, Maria. *Secrets from the Grave*. New York: St. Martin's, 1998.

Felsenthal, Edward. "Was Lawyer Shot by Doctor? Case Portrays Twisted Loyalty." *Wall Street Journal*, July 2, 1996. http://www.wsj.com/articles/SB836261211616141000.

"Prosecutor: Doctor in Love Triangle Killed Friend to Marry Wife." *Daily American*, March 4, 2008. http://articles.dailyamerican.com/2008-03-04/news/26324545_1_scher-martin-dillon-skeet-shooting.

Wilkinson, Alec. "A Gun Shot." *Esquire*, January 29, 2007. https://www.esquire.com/news-politics/a1795/gun-shot-0200/.

Wilson, Staci. "Scher Dies in Prison." *Susquehanna County Independent*, October 20, 2010. http://www.susqcoindy.com/PS/2010/10/20/scher-dies-in-prison/.

FROM THE *CHARLOTTE OBSERVER* (IN CHRONOLOGICAL ORDER):

Wilson, Chip. "Lincolnton Man Dares Officials to Charge Him in 1976 Killing." June 28, 1994, 1A.

———. "2 Jurors Picked for Doctor's Murder Trial." September 11, 1997, 3C.

———. "Prosecutor Keeps Pressure on Dr. Scher." October 8, 1997, 6C.

Tomlinson, Tommy. "Did Change of Heart Make Story Change?" October 8, 1997, 1C.

Wilson, Chip. "21 Years Later, Scher Guilty." October 23, 1997, 1A.

———. "Prosecutor: Scher's Trial 'A 50-50 Shot'." October 24, 1997, 1A.

Zielinski, Michel Eleanor. "Judge Drops Perjury Charges Filed against Patricia Scher." May 23, 1998, 1C.

Cataldo, Adam, and Joe DePriest. "Scher Returns to Prison to Resume Life Sentence." August 23, 2002, 1A.

Rubinkam, Michael. "Scher Convicted in '76 Killings: 2nd Trial in Shotgun Slaying of Best Friend." March 14, 2008, 1B.

CHAPTER 4

"Barbara Brewton Cameron Dies in Florida." Q City Metro, December 7, 2008. https://qcitymetro.com/2008/12/07/barbara-brewton-cameron-died-in-florida-083118965/.

"Bikers Pay Respects at Funeral." *Charlotte Observer*, October 2, 1981, 1A.

Brachey, Nancy. "Graham Day Hearing Begins with Anthem." *Charlotte Observer*, February 29, 1972, 4A.

Cherrie, Victoria. "The Secret Life of HushHush." EyeCharlotte, December 2008/January 2009, 26–27.

Clark, Robin, and Tex O'Neill. "A Biker's Lonely Quest That Ended in Brutal Death." *Charlotte Observer*, November 1, 1981, 1A.

———. "Outnumbered and Outsmarted, Police Can't Keep Pace." *Charlotte Observer*, August 20, 1981, 1A.

———. "Those Who Join: Experts Say 'Urban Outlaws' Are Not as Different from Outsiders as They Might Seem." *Charlotte Observer*, Aug. 19, 1981.

———. "Women along for the Ride: They Stay Despite Abuse." *Charlotte Observer*, August 19, 1981, 1A.

Clark, Robin, Tex O'Neill, and Katherine White. "Suspect Denies Guilt in '79 Biker Killings." *Charlotte Observer*, November 17, 1981, 1A.

DeAngelis, Mary Elizabeth. "Indictment Says Pair Ran Prostitution Ring." *Charlotte Observer*, July 13, 1995, 1A.

Dyer, Leigh. "Mystery of 1979 Biker Massacre Still Unsolved." *Charlotte Observer*, July 3, 1999, 1A.

Elder, Jeff. "Blessed by the Peace Maker: Pastor Barbara Cameron Stood Up to Gangs, Guns and Drugs to Change Life in Genesis Park." *Charlotte Observer*, May 11, 2008, 1E.

Gary, Kays. "Near Kiss to NASCAR." *Charlotte Observer*, November 13, 2009.

George, Jefferson. "Money Trail, Trash, Laptop Build Case on Sex Business." *Charlotte Observer*, December 7, 2007, 1A.

Hackman, John, and David Perlmutt. "A Show That Marshville Won't Soon Forget." *Charlotte Observer*, October 2, 1981, 12A.

Kay, Lindell. "Biker Slayings Remain Mystery." *Asheboro Courier-Tribune*, December 26, 2014. http://www.courier-tribune.com/news/local/ramseur-biker-slayings-remain-mystery.

Kelley, Pam. *Money Rock: A Family's Story of Cocaine, Race, and Ambition in the New South*. New York: The New Press, 2018.

Lavigne, Yves. *Hell's Angels: "Three Can Keep a Secret if Two are Dead."* 62–63, 324–25. New York: Carol Publishing, 1987, 1995.

McClain, Kathleen. "Drug Dealer Gets Life Plus 45 Years." *Charlotte Observer*, August 8, 1995, 1C.

Mellnik, Ted. "11 Indicted as Cleanup of Kenney St. Begins." *Charlotte Observer*, February 8, 1992, 1C.

Norwood, Allen. "Crowd Outnumbers Bikers at Hell's Angels' Funeral." *Charlotte Observer*, October 2, 1981, 1A.

Petersen, Bo. "Bikers Brought Turf Wars, Drugs to Gaston." *Gaston Gazette*, May 22, 1993. Retrieved from *Greensboro News & Record*.

Smith, Gail. "Good Day for Selling Hamburgers." *Charlotte Observer*, October 2, 1981.

Sparrow v. Goodman, 361 F.Supp. 566 (W.D.N.C. 1973) [Red Hornet Mayday Tribe case.]

Washburn, Mark. "How Police Solved 1979 Biker Massacre." *Charlotte Observer*, July 8, 2015.

———. "Inside the Investigation of Charlotte's Worst Mass Killing." *Charlotte Observer*, July 3, 2016, 25A.

Weinstein, Michael. "13 of 60 Bikers Ticketed for Riding without Helmets." *Charlotte Observer*, October 2, 1981.

Wicker, Ann. "Draggin' The Tourist Line: From What Might Have Been to What We Have Left." *Creative Loafing Charlotte*, March 19, 2004. https://clclt.com/charlotte/draggin-the-tourist-line/Content?oid=2354287.

Wildman, John. "Angels' Funeral Respectful." *Charlotte Observer*, October 2, 1981, 6A.

Wright, Gary L. "Feds: Sex Ring Made Millions." *Charlotte Observer*, November 16, 2007, 1B.

———. "Sex-Ring Madam Given 2-Year Term." *Charlotte Observer*, August 27, 2008.

Chapter 5

"Ex-Monroe Police Officer Confessed to Murder." *Star News Online*, July 22, 2005. http://www.starnewsonline.com/news/20050722/ex-monroe-police-officer-confessed-to-murder.

Forensic Files, "Traffic Violations." May 8, 2008.

"Murder Jury Was Split over Sentence." *Greensboro News & Record*, March 5, 1998. https://www.greensboro.com/murder-jury-was-split-over-sentence/article_18e44e21-82ad-5f2e-ae66-cb9c3f52466f.html.

NC v. Griffin, No. COA99-140 (NC Court of Appeals opinion, February 15, 2000).

Six Degrees of Murder, "A Deadly Drive." July 13, 2016.

FROM THE *CHARLOTTE OBSERVER* (IN CHRONOLOGICAL ORDER):

Banchero, Stephanie. "Slain Woman Buried: Police Still Seek Killer." April 4, 1997, 1C.

———. "Rumors Fly in Medlin Murder Case." April 6, 1997, 1B.

LaPolla, Joie. "Woman Was Strangled, Had Other Injuries, Too, Autopsy Report Says." May 28, 1997, 2C.

———. "Officer Charged with Murder." May 31, 1997, 1A.

———. "Medlin Evidence Unsealed: Human Blood, Hair Found in Police Car." June 3, 1997, 1A.

Powell, Dannye Romine. "Griffin's Day in Court—and Medlin's." June 3, 1997, 1C.

———. "DA Seeking Death Penalty in Medlin Slaying." June 4, 1997, 1A.

Griffin, Anna. "Friend Stands behind Griffin Despite Arrest." June 4, 1997, 13A.

LaPolla, Joie. "Lawyer Demands Access to Evidence: Death Penalty Asked for Ex-Officer Charged with Woman's Abduction, Slaying." July 31, 1997, 1C.

Perlmutt, David, and Wendy Goodman. "Dogs Found No Body, Witnesses Say." February 14, 1998, 1C.

CHAPTER 6

Friedland v. Gales, COA98-367. https://caselaw.findlaw.com/nc-court-of-appeals/1049284.html.

Johnston, Lori. "How Does This Man Sleep at Night?" *Charlotte Magazine*, 2003. https://rudolfwidenhouse.com/wp-content/uploads/2013/07/How-Does-This-Man-Sleep-at-Night.pdf.

Klein, Jerry. "Rush to Judgment." *Creative Loafing Charlotte*, March 7, 1997. https://www.siliconinvestor.com/readmsg.aspx?msgid=15078133.

Lewis, Cynthia. "Either/Or." *Charlotte Magazine*, June and July 2006. http://www.charlottemagazine.com/Charlotte-Magazine/June-2006/Either-Or/.

Murder Accountability Project. www.murderdata.org/p/blog-page.html.

Servatius, Tara. "The One That Got Away: Who Killed Kim Thomas?" *Creative Loafing Charlotte*, August 13, 2008, 16.

FROM THE *CHARLOTTE OBSERVER* (IN CHRONOLOGICAL ORDER):

DeAngelis, Mary Elizabeth. "Husband Charged in '90 Slaying of Activist Kim Thomas." July 12, 1994, 1A.

———. "Couple a Picture of Success before Killing." July 17, 1994, 1B.

McClain, Kathleen. "Pathologist Reviews Evidence." March 21, 1995, 1C.

———. "Friedland Murder Charge Dropped." March 29, 1995, 1A.

Leland, Elizabeth. "Who Killed Kim Thomas?" July 30–August 2, 1995.

———. "New Leads Traced in '90 Murder." September 3, 1995, 1B.

———. "MD Accuses Inmate of Killing Wife." March 30, 1996, 1C.

———. "Kim Thomas Crime-Scene Procedures Questioned." March 4, 1997, 1A.

Wright, Gary L. "Police Say Court Barred Release of Thomas Info." March 11, 1997, 3C.

Leland, Elizabeth. "Kim Thomas' Husband Guests on Radio Show." March 11, 1997, 1C.

———. "Friedland Suit Alleges Police Malice in Thomas Case." June 4, 1997, 1C.

———. "Shooting by Gales Is Admissible." September 9, 1997, 1C.

Leland, Elizabeth, and Foon Rhee. "Death Suit Target Secures Legal Help." September 10, 1997, 1C.

Leland, Elizabeth. "Lawyers Try to Shift Suspicion in Slaying." September 11, 1997, 1C.

———. "Wrongful-Death Jury Told of Man's Threats, Crimes." September 12, 1997, 2C.

———. "Evidence at Scene of Crime Is Focus." September 13, 1997, 1C.

Price, Mark. "In Video, Gales Says Many Witnesses Lied." September 17, 1997, 1C.

Leland, Elizabeth. "Doctor: Slaying Was Start of 'Long Road.'" September 18, 1997, 1A.

———. "Jurors Hear Excerpts from Murder Victim's Journal." September 20, 1997, 1C.

Price, Mark. "Suspect in '90 Case Accused in New Killing." July 23, 2008, 1A.

Lacour, Greg, and Gary L. Wright. "New Hope of Solving '90 Killing." August 20, 2008, 1A.

Wootson, Cleve, Jr., and Elizabeth Leland. "Probe of 1990 Killing Widens." February 18, 2010, 1A.

Leland, Elizabeth. "Police Looking at 'Person of Interest' in Murder Case." March 3, 2010, 1B.

Leland, Elizabeth. "Friends, Family Recall Woman Slain in 1990." September 8, 2013, 1B.

CHAPTER 7

The Charley Project. "Asha Jaquilla Degree" (updated February 27, 2018). http://charleyproject.org/case/asha-jaquilla-degree.

Crosland, Sarah. "A Slice of History Found at Open Kitchen." *Charlotte Magazine*, May 30, 2018. http://www.charlottemagazine.com/Charlotte-Magazine/June-2018/A-Slice-of-History-Found-at-Open-Kitchen/.

DePriest, Joe. "Old Mystery Leads Retired Detective to Mount Holly." *Charlotte Observer*, October 21, 2014, 1A.

DePriest, Joe, and Steve Lyttle. "After 13 Years, Police Still Looking for Asha Degree." *Charlotte Observer*, February 14, 2013.

Douglas, John, and Mark Olshaker. *Mind Hunter: Inside the FBI's Elite Serial Crime Unit*. New York: Scribner, 1995.

Dr. Phil. "Erica Parsons." August 20 and August 21, 2013.

Dys, Andrew. "The Genesis of a Murderer." *Rock Hill Herald*, October 20, 2007. https://www.heraldonline.com/news/local/news-columns-blogs/andrew-dys/article12194075.html.

"Finding Asha Degree, Shelby's Sweetheart." https://findingashadegree.wordpress.com.

Garfield, Ken, and Joe DePriest. "Lost Faces of Charlotte." *Charlotte Magazine*, August 2016, 72–75.

Hinton, John. "WFU Grad Missing for 37 Years Identified with DNA, Dental Records." *Winston-Salem Journal*, October 31, 2012.

The Kristen Foundation. http://www.kristenfoundation.org/.

Moffitt, Mike. "Potential Lead in Kristen Modafferi Cold Case Goes Uninvestigated." SFGATE, June 22, 2018. https://www.sfgate.com/local/article/Kristen-Modafferi-cold-case-Oakland-Jayne-DNA-13005068.php.

———. "What Happened to Kristen Modafferi? One Man's Search for Answers in San Francisco Cold Case." SFGATE, June 21, 2018. https://www.sfgate.com/local/article/Kristen-Modafferi-Dennis-Mahon-Onuma-missing-Lampo-12988187.php.

Monument Multi-Media. *Anatomy: Cold Case Atlanta, Case: 16854, Diane Shields.* https://monumentmultimedia.com/showcase/cold-case-atlanta-diane-shields/.

———. *Anatomy: Cold Case Atlanta, Case: 43279, Mary Shotwell Little.* https://monumentmultimedia.com/showcase/cold-case-atlanta-mary-shotwell-little/.

Moore, Kylie. "3 of the Most Fascinating Unsolved Cases in Charlotte History." *Charlotte Agenda*, January 31, 2017. https://www.charlotteagenda.com/76150/unsolved-cases-cmpd/.

National Missing and Unidentified Persons Systems. https://www.namus.gov.

Price, Mark. "Adoptive Parents Indicted in Killing of Erica Parsons." *Charlotte Observer*, February 21, 2018, 1A.

Scott, Susan Carpenter. maryshotwelllittle.blogspot.com.

Shuler, Rita. *Carolina Crimes: Case Files of a Forensic Photographer*. Charleston, SC: The History Press, 2006.

———. *Murder in the Midlands: 28 Days of Terror that Shook South Carolina*. Charleston, SC: The History Press, 2007.

State v. Head, 79 N.C. App. 1, 338 S.E.2d 908 (N.C. Ct. App. 1986).

Washburn, Mark. "Missing Nearly Five Years, Erica Parsons Found Buried in Rural S.C." *Charlotte Observer*, September 29, 2016. www.charlotteobserver.com/news/local/crime/article105048256.html.

Wester, Jane. "Prosecutors Will Seek Death Penalty for Both of Erica Parsons' Adoptive Parents." *Charlotte Observer*, April 12, 2018. www.charlotteobserver.com/news/local/crime/article208673534.html.

Wilmer, Harry. "Murder Most Foul: Charlotte's Unsolved Homicides." *Charlotte Magazine*, September 1984, 16–17, 35.

Wootson, Cleve R. "Missing Woman from '75 ID'd." *Charlotte Observer*, November 2, 2012, 1B.

CHAPTER 8

Dateline NBC. "Mystery on the Catawba River." July 9, 2011.

Free Mark Carver. http://FreeMarkCarver.com.

Gordon, Michael. "Attorneys Say Investigators Ignored 2 Potential Suspects in Ira Yarmolenko Murder." *Charlotte Observer*, July 26, 2018, 1A.

———. "Carver's Attorneys: Why Did Missing Files Wind Up with the Prosecutor?" *Charlotte Observer*, September 11, 2017, 1A.

———. "Carver's Defense Team Wants Gaston DA Held in contempt." *Charlotte Observer*, June 15, 2017, 11A.

———. "Judge Orders DNA to Undergo State Lab Analysis." *Charlotte Observer*, April 21, 2017, 1A.

———. "Lawyer Requested a New Trial for Mark Carver." *Charlotte Observer*, December 10, 2016, 1A.

Himmelreich, Claudia. "Germany's Phantom Serial Killer: A DNA Blunder." March 27, 2009. http://content.time.com/time/world/article/0,8599,1888126,00.html.

Kaplan, Tracey. "Monte Sereno Murder Casts Doubt on DNA Evidence." *Mercury News*, June 28, 2014 (updated August 12, 2016). https://www.mercurynews.com/2014/06/28/monte-sereno-murder-case-casts-doubts-on-dna-evidence/.

Kratt, Mary. *Charlotte, North Carolina: A Brief History*. Charleston, SC: The History Press, 2009.

Lawson, Adam. "Judge Grants Mark Carver New Trial in Ira Yarmolenko Killing." *Gaston Gazette*, June 5, 2019. https://www.gastongazette.com/news/20190605/judge-grants-mark-carver-new-trial-in-ira-yarmolenko-killing.

Leland, Elizabeth. "Death by the River." *Charlotte Observer*, April 3–8, 2016.

20/20. "The Mark Carver Case." December 9, 2016.

[For more on cutting-edge DNA science and the hunt for the East Area Rapist/Golden State Killer, see *I'll Be Gone in the Dark: One Woman's Obsessive Search for the Golden State Killer* (New York: Harper, 2018) by Michelle McNamara; despite her forward-thinking work using genetic databases, the author died two years before Joseph James DeAngelo was identified using familial DNA and captured.

For more on DNA exonerations in the United States, see the Innocence Project (https://www.innocenceproject.org/dna-exonerations-in-the-united-states/).]

Chapter 9

The Bhagwan

Bovsun, Mara. "750 Sickened in Oregon Restaurants as Cult Known as the Rajneeshees Spread Salmonella in Town of The Dalles: Salad-Bar Attack by Followers of Bhagwan Shree Rajneesh Was the Largest Act of Bioterrorism on U.S. Soil." *New York Daily News*, June 15, 2013.

Douglas, Anna. "He Was Captured in the Middle of the Night on a Charlotte Runway. Now It's on Netflix." *Charlotte Observer*, April 23, 2018.

McCormack, Win. *The Rajneesh Chronicles: The True Story of the Cult that Unleashed the First Act of Bioterrorism on U.S. Soil*. Portland and New York: Tin House Books, 2010.

Morrill, Jim. "Bhagwan a Chapter in 'Amazing Life'—Charlotte Woman Was Bystander for Arrest of Fugitive Guru in 1985." *Charlotte Observer*, November 10, 2005, 3B.

Paddock, Polly. "The Right Man for the Job." *Charlotte Observer*, November 24, 1985, 1B.

Purvis, Kathleen. "Welcome to—Livermush Land." *Charlotte Observer*, October 18, 2000, 1E.

"Rajneeshees: An *Oregonian* Special Report." *The Oregonian*, June 30, 1985. https://www.oregonlive.com/pacific-northwest-news/index.ssf/2018/03/read_the_oregonians_original_2.html.

Török, Thomas J., Robert V. Tauxe, Robert P. Wise, John R. Livengood, Robert Sokolow, Steven Mauvais, Kristin A. Birkness, Michael R. Skeels, John M. Horan and Laurence R. Foster. "A Large Community Outbreak of Salmonellosis Caused by Intentional Contamination of Restaurant Salad Bars." *Journal of the American Medical Assn.* Vol. 278, no. 5 (August 6, 1997): 389–95. https://www.cdc.gov/phlp/docs/forensic_epidemiology/Additional%20Materials/Articles/Torok%20et%20al.pdf.

Wild Wild Country. Maclain Way and Chapman Way, directors. Netflix, 2018.

Wines, Michael, and Russell Chandler. "Guru, 8 Followers Jailed after Cross-Country Flight." *Los Angeles Times*, October 29, 1985. http://articles.latimes.com/1985-10-29/news/mn-13045_1_bhagwan-shree-rajneesh.

Wollaston, Sam. "Growing Up in the Wild Wild Country Cult: 'You Heard People Having Sex All the Time, Like Baboons.'" *The Guardian*, April 24, 2018. https://www.theguardian.com/tv-and-radio/2018/apr/24/wild-wild-country-netflix-cult-sex-noa-maxwell-bhagwan-shree-rajneesh-commune-childhood.

Zaitz, Les. "25 Years after Rajneeshee Commune Collapsed, Truth Spills Out." *The Oregonian* and *OregonLive*, April 14, 2011 (updated February 18, 2014). https://www.oregonlive.com/rajneesh/index.ssf/page/post.html.

Viktor Gunnarsson

"Court Upholds Murder Conviction of L.C. Underwood." *Watauga Democrat*, January 19, 2011. https://www.wataugademocrat.com/news/court-upholds-murder-conviction-of-l-c-underwood/article_707f4c42-2616-5096-9d17-73d39c2f4dbd.html.

Forensic Files, "To the Viktor." June 14, 2006.

Mitchell, Monte. "Retrial Granted in Killing of Swede." *Winston-Salem Journal*, January 19, 2010. https://www.journalnow.com/news/local/retrial-granted-in-killing-of-swede/article_8d93d4ac-5db1-54a7-832b-3fcbac562681.html.

North Carolina v. Lamont Claxton Underwood, 518 S.E.2d 231 (N.C. Ct. App. 1999), cert. denied as improvidently granted, 535 S.E.2d 33 (N.C. 2000).

Pickens, Cathy. "Politics and Conspiracies." *Mystery Readers Journal*, Scandinavian Mysteries I, 23:3, 2007.

———. "A Top-Ten Unsolved Murder." *Mystery Readers Journal*, Scandinavian Mysteries II, 31:2, 2014.

Ramsey, Robin. Review of *Blood on the Snow: The Killing of Olof Palme* by Jan Bondeson. Cornell, 2005.

Smith, Gail, and Anna Griffin. "Former Officer Is Charged in Slaying." *Charlotte Observer*, October 13, 1995, 1C.

Underwood v. Harkelroad, U.S. 4th Cir., No. 10-6077, 2011 (unpublished opinion). https://www.gpo.gov/fdsys/pkg/USCOURTS-ca4-10-06077/pdf/USCOURTS-ca4-10-06077-0.pdf.

Gregory Caplinger

Barrett, Stephen, M.D. "Gregory Caplinger and His Cancer Scam." www.Quackwatch.org, July 12, 2009. http://www.quackwatch.org/01QuackeryRelatedTopics/Cancer/immustim.html.

Davant, Charles III, M.D. "Why I Carry a Gun." *Medical Economics*, 80:43, December 5, 2003.

U.S. v. Caplinger, 339 F. 3d 226 (4th Cir. 2003).

CHAPTER 10

Related to Frank Littlejohn

Doster, Joe. "Frank Littlejohn Dead at Age 80." *Charlotte Observer*, November 29, 1965.

"Editorial: The Littlejohn Episode." *Charlotte Observer*, September 8, 1940.

Hoover, Harry. "America's Finest Detective." *The State*, July 1990, 10–11.

————. "The Greatest Charlotte Crime Story You've Probably Never Heard." *Charlotte Five*, March 7, 2017. https://www.charlottefive.com/big-crime-in-the-little-city/.

Kilgo, John. "City's 'Best Known' Chief Dies." *Charlotte News*, November 29, 1965, 1B.

————. "Crimes of the Century." *Charlotte News*, Robinson-Spangler Carolina Room, Charlotte-Mecklenburg Public Library vertical file; no date on clipping.

————. "Frank Littlejohn: A Genuine Man." *Charlotte News*, November 29, 1965.

————. "Soft as Putty Or Hard as Rock: A Visit with Ex-Chief Littlejohn." *Charlotte News*, June 11, 1960.

"Roger 'The Terrible' Touhy." https://www.fbi.gov/history/famous-cases/roger-the-terrible-touhy.

State v. Dale, 218 N.C. 625, 12 S.E.2d 556 (1940).

Summerville, Diane. "Charlotte's Crime of the Century." *Our State Magazine*, December 15, 2010.

Wilmer, Harry. "America's Finest Detective: Frank Littlejohn—A Chief to Remember." *Charlotte Magazine*, February [no year on copy], 32.

FROM THE *CHARLOTTE OBSERVER* COVERAGE OF THE DALE-WISHART TRIAL (IN CHRONOLOGICAL ORDER):

"Stenographic Report of Testimony at Dale-Wishart Trial." August 15, 1940.

"Jury Clears Dr. Wishart and Finds Dales Guilty." August 23, 1940, 17.

"Expect Action to Take Place on Wednesday." September 10, 1940, 23–24.

"Dale-Wishart Case Is Linked with Littlejohn Hearing." September 27, 1940, 21–22.

"Three Charges Against Littlejohn Are Dismissed." October 29, 1940, 13, 15.

"Littlejohn Is Dismissed by Board on Vote of 2 to 1." November 2, 1940, 13, 15.

"Fred Dale Now in County Jail." November 5, 1940, 7.

Related to Garry McFadden

TELEVISION AND RADIO:

Bad Henry. Investigation Discovery, July 24, 2018.

Charlotte Talks. "Charlotte and Mecklenburg County Police History." WFAE Mike Collins interview, http://www.wfae.org/post/charlotte-and-mecklenburg-county-police-history.

"Every Detective Starts as a Rookie." Garry McFadden on Investigation Discovery podcast episode 2-01. http://crimefeed.com/2016/06/detective-podcast-season-2-episode-1/.

I Am Homicide. Investigation Discovery series, 2016 (season 1), 2017 (season 2).

BOOKS AND ARTICLES:

Bolling, Cristina. "The Fashion Police: 5 Style Lessons from a Former CMPD Homicide Cop—Who's Also a Fashionista." *Charlotte Observer*, August 6, 2017, 1C.

Cain, Brooke. "He Was One of the Best Homicide Detectives in NC. Now He Has His Own True Crime TV Show." *Raleigh News & Observer*, August 14, 2017. https://www.newsobserver.com/entertainment/tv/warm-tv-blog/article167063617.html.

———. "New Documentary Focuses on Famous Charlotte Killer." *Charlotte Observer*, July 24, 2018.

Coston, Charisse T.M., and Joseph B. Kuhns, III. "Lives Interrupted!: A Case Study of Henry Louis Wallace—an African-American Serial Murderer in a Rapidly Expanding Southern City." *Free Inquiry in Creative Sociology*, 32:2, November 2, 2004, 141–150. https://pages.uncc.edu/ccoston/wp-content/uploads/sites/10/2011/09/LivesInterrupted.pdf.

DeAngelis, Mary Elizabeth. "Henry Louis Wallace: Portrait of a Charmer." *Charlotte Observer*, March 20, 1994, 1A.

———. "Police Deny Race Delayed Arrest, But Changes Are Made." *Charlotte Observer*, September 29, 1996, 21A.

———. "Victim's Dad Says Arrests a Big Relief." *Charlotte Observer*, March 29, 1996, 1C.

Garfield, Ken, and Henry Eichel. "Man Charged with 10 Murders." *Charlotte Observer*, March 14, 1994, 1A.

Geringer, Joseph. "Henry Louis Wallace." Crime Library, http://www.trutv.com. https://pages.uncc.edu/ccoston/wp-content/uploads/sites/10/2011/09/Henry_Louis_Wallace_ccrime_library.pdf.

Lapeyre, Jason. "The Serial Killer the Cops Ignored: The Henry Louis Wallace Murders." October 14, 2009. http://murderpedia.org/male.W/w/wallace-henry-louis.htm.

McClain, Kathleen. "The Wallace File." *Charlotte Observer*, September 29, 1996, 20A.

McShane, Chuck. "1993: Charlotte's Deadliest Year." *Charlotte Magazine*, November 21, 2013. http://www.charlottemagazine.com/Charlotte-Magazine/December-2013/1993-Charlottes-Deadliest-Year/.

Mothers of Murdered Offspring. https://momocares.org.

Pierre, Milca. "Investigation Discovery's New Series 'I Am Homicide' to Document Garry McFadden, Detective Who's Worked 700 Cases." June 14, 2016. http://thesource.com/2016/06/14/investigation-discoverys-new-series-i-am-homicide-to-document-garry-mcfadden-detective-whos-worked-700-cases/.

Price, Mark. "Charlotte Is on the List of 'Deadliest U.S. Cities.'" *Charlotte Observer*, February 12, 2018.

Washburn, Mark. "TV's 'I Am Homicide' to Capture Career of Charlotte's Oddball Detective." *Charlotte Observer*, June 10, 2016. http://www.charlotteobserver.com/entertainment/tv/media-scene-blog/article83038492.html.

Wiest, Julie Bethany. Dissertation: "Creating Cultural Monsters: A Critical Analysis of the Representation of Serial Murderers in America." University of Tennessee, May 2009. http://citeseerx.ist.psu.edu/viewdoc/download?doi=10.1.1.428.4224&rep=rep1&type=pdf.

Wright, Angela. "Slain Man Planned Life Helping Others." *Charlotte Observer*, November 9, 1993, 1C.

Wright, Gary, and Cleve R. Wootson, Jr. "The McFadden File." *Charlotte Observer*, June 10, 2016. http://www.charlotteobserver.com/entertainment/tv/media-scene-blog/article83038492.html.

ABOUT THE AUTHOR

Courtesy of Libby Dickinson.

Cathy Pickens, a lawyer and college professor, is a crime fiction writer (*Southern Fried Mysteries*, St. Martin's/ Minotaur) and true-crime columnist for *Mystery Readers Journal*. She taught law in the McColl School of Business and served as provost at Queens University of Charlotte; she also served as national president of Sisters in Crime and on the boards of Mystery Writers of America and the Mecklenburg Forensic Medicine Program (an evidence collection/preservation training collaborative).

Currently, she offers workshops on developing the creative process, coaches and teaches new writers through Charlotte Lit and works with former inmates on starting their own businesses and writing their own stories.